The Dynamics of the Price Structure and the Business Cycle

Contributions to Economics

http://www.springer.de/cgi-bin/search_book.pl?series=1262

Further volumes of this series can be found at our homepage.

Friedel Bolle/Michael Carlberg (Eds.)
Advances in Behavioral Economics
2001. ISBN 3-7908-1358-3

Volker Grossmann
Inequality, Economic Growth, and Technological Change
2001. ISBN 3-7908-1364-8

Thomas Riechmann
Learning in Economics
2001. ISBN 3-7908-1384-2

Miriam Beblo
Bargaining over Time Allocation
2001. ISBN 3-7908-1391-5

Peter Meusburger/Heike Jöns (Eds.)
Transformations in Hungary
2001. ISBN 3-7908-1412-1

Claus Brand
Money Stock Control and Inflation Targeting in Germany
2001. ISBN 3-7908-1393-1

Erik Lüth
Private Intergenerational Transfers and Population Aging
2001. ISBN 3-7908-1402-4

Nicole Pohl
Mobility in Space and Time
2001. ISBN 3-7908-1380-X

Pablo Coto-Millán (Ed.)
Essays on Microeconomics and Industrial Organisation
2002. ISBN 3-7908-1390-7

Mario A. Maggioni
Clustering Dynamics and the Locations of High-Tech-Firms
2002. ISBN 3-7908-1431-8

Ludwig Schätzl/Javier Revilla Diez (Eds.)
Technological Change and Regional Development in Europe
2002. ISBN 3-7908-1460-1

Alberto Quadrio Curzio/Marco Fortis (Eds.)
Complexity and Industrial Clusters
2002. ISBN 3-7908-1471-7

Friedel Bolle/Marco Lehmann-Waffenschmidt (Eds.)
Surveys in Experimental Economics
2002. ISBN 3-7908-1472-5

Pablo Coto-Millán
General Equilibrium and Welfare
2002. ISBN 7908-1491-1

Wojciech W. Charemza/Krystyna Strzala (Eds.)
East European Transition and EU Enlargement
2002. ISBN 3-7908-1501-2

Natalja von Westernhagen
Systemic Transformation, Trade and Economic Growth
2002. ISBN 3-7908-1521-7

Josef Falkinger
A Theory of Employment in Firms
2002. ISBN 3-7908-1520-9

Engelbert Plassmann
Econometric Modelling of European Money Demand
2003. ISBN 3-7908-1522-5

Reginald Loyen/Erik Buyst/Greta Devos (Eds.)
Struggeling for Leadership: Antwerp-Rotterdam Port Competition between 1870–2000
2003. ISBN 3-7908-1524-1

Pablo Coto-Millán
Utility and Production, 2nd Edition
2003. ISBN 3-7908-1423-7

Emilio Colombo/John Driffill (Eds.)
The Role of Financial Markets in the Transition Process
2003. ISBN 3-7908-0004-X

Guido S. Merzoni
Strategic Delegation in Firms and in the Trade Union
2003. ISBN 3-7908-1432-6

Jan B. Kuné
On Global Aging
2003. ISBN 3-7908-0030-9

Sugata Marjit, Rajat Acharyya
International Trade, Wage Inequality and the Developing Economy
2003. ISBN 3-7908-0031-7

Francesco C. Billari/Alexia Prskawetz (Eds.)
Agent-Based Computational Demography
2003. ISBN 3-7908-1550-0

Georg Bol/Gholamreza Nakhaeizadeh/Svetlozar T. Rachev/Thomas Ridder/Karl-Heinz Vollmer (Eds.)
Credit Risk
2003. ISBN 3-7908-0054-6

Christian Müller
Money Demand in Europe
2003. ISBN 3-7908-0064-3

Cristina Nardi Spiller

The Dynamics of the Price Structure and the Business Cycle

The Italian Evidence from 1945 to 2000

Physica-Verlag
A Springer-Verlag Company

Series Editors
Werner A. Müller
Martina Bihn

Author

Associated Prof. Cristina Nardi Spiller
Department of Economics
University of Verona
Via dell'Artigliere 19
37129 Verona
Italy
cristina.spiller@univr.it

ISSN 1431-1933
ISBN 3-7908-0063-5 Physica-Verlag Heidelberg New York

Library of Congress Cataloging-in-Publication Data
Nardi Spiller, Cristina.
The dynamics of the price structure and the business cycle: the Italian evidence from 1945–2000 / Cristina Nardi Spiller.
p. cm. – (Contributions to economics)
ISBN 3-7908-0063-5 (softcover: alk. paper)
1. Business cycles–Italy–History–20th century. 2. Prices–Italy. 3. Italy–Economic policy. 4. Italy–Economic conditions–1945- I. Title. II. Series.

Physica-Verlag Heidelberg New York
a member of BertelsmannSpringer Science+Business Media GmbH

http://www.springer.de

Softcover Design: Erich Kirchner, Heidelberg

SPIN 10924952 88/3130/DK-5 4 3 2 1 0 – Printed on acid-free and non-aging paper

To Marina Bagnani Querena

Without you, the beauty of spring has gone

I save special thanks for Mauro Baranzini, whose detailed comments on parts of this book have improved it considerably. Thanks also to Nicola Gelder for helping me with the translation. I thank my students for their encouragement and finally I would like to thank my husband for his suggestions and for understanding my task.

[...] are the monetary and credit phenomena which arise during the business cycle the cause of the phenomena relating to production and the circulation of goods, or are they rather the effect?
(Bresciani Turroni, 1951, p. 133)

Foreword

In an economy the price level not only represents the value of a good or service, it also reflects the state of the economy. Low prices might discourage supply, which is no longer motivated by potential returns, and lead to a lower rate of output and a lower level of employment. In turn demand will be conditioned by the inferior level of real income, and undoubtedly will no longer be able to "pull" the economy. Thus effective demand plays a crucial role, and insufficient demand may cause an alarming situation: one possible Keynesian recipe for which is deficit spending. Indeed deficit spending is often considered a panacea and adopted irresponsibly, to the detriment of state balances and with little hope of restoring economic activity.

Conversely in a state of rapidly rising prices, demand is less elastic and as expectations of further price rises grow, goods become progressively more expensive. Consumers, who are highly sensitive to changes in their income, are less attentive to changes in the price level. Attempts made by consumers to restore or even increase their income by demanding wage increases may result in inevitable increases in labour costs (in the absence of a corresponding increase in productivity). This in turn may induce entrepreneurs to attempt to restore or increase their profits, fostering the onset of risky «mark-up battles» (Fellner, 1959).

The interrelationships which exist in the various markets produce a number of mechanisms, which in turn create complex situations. Inflation may subsist below the full-employment level, but it may also emerge in conditions of over-employment of factors of production, despite equilibrium in the markets for goods and services. It may even emerge where there is an excess supply of the goods and services.

Inflationary impulses may stem from an increase in the supply of money, from a fall in the liquidity preference, from a decrease in supply of goods, services and inputs, from rising production costs not matched by a corresponding increase in productivity, or from policy choices themselves.

Inflation may develop gradually before exploding, or it may appear suddenly. The price to be paid for overcoming the distortion may not be immediately evident: the often serious consequences may be passed on to subsequent time periods, as the phenomenon of hysteresis (in which the past value of a variable influences the present value of the same variable) clearly shows. In this way the target of price stability becomes more elusive. Attempts to reach such a target are hindered by badly timed and poorly focused interventions and indeed failure is often the result of ill-constructed, uncoordinated measures applied to different markets at different times. Measures to deflate prices may have a negative impact on the level of employment: indeed the term deflation is often used as a synonym of recession.

In the last century Italy was characterised by the North-South gap, and other less blatant but nevertheless material geographical imbalances. The existence of a significant technological gap, the alternating bargaining power of trade unions, and the presence of several different market forms also contributed to the fragile state of the country. In such a situation it was not possible to formulate instant recipes for easily attainable results.

Here we wish to examine the experience of the Italian economy in the light of the most important international events. We will do this within a long-term analytical framework, and with reference to the principal theoretical approaches. Our analysis seeks to interpret events in the economy, recorded over time, with particular emphasis on price dynamics. We aim to understand the origins of these processes, investigate their impact and evaluate both positive and negative aspects of policy measures. An important implication of such an approach is that it leads us to assess the different aspects of the evolution of the Italian economic structure, analysing the dynamic behaviour of policy makers and social partners. In doing so we are aware that the present situation has both benefited from and been disadvantaged by policies from the recent, and indeed the more distant past.

Cristina Nardi Spiller
Università di Verona, Italy, February 2003

Contents

1. The Italian Economy in the Immediate Post-War Period

2. The Great Leap and the Subsequent U-Turn

List of Abbreviations

AGIP	Italian Petroleum Company
AIMA	Public Corporation Responsible for Managing Agricultural Markets
AM-lire	Allied Military Currency
ANAS	Highways Agency
APSM	Agency for the Promotion and Development of the Mezzo-giorno
BI	Bank of Italy
CGIL	General Confederation of Italian Trade Unions
CICR	Interdepartmental Committee on Credit and Saving
CIF	Cost, Insurance and Freight
CIG	Dole and Welfare Benefits
CIP	Interdepartmental Committee on Prices
CIPE	Interdepartmental Committee for Economic Planning
CISL	Italian Federation of Trade Unions
CLUP	Cost of Labour per Unit of Product
COLA	Cost of Living Adjustment
DCE	Domestic Credit Expansion
EC	European Comunity
ECB	European Central Bank
ECSC	European Coal and Steel Community
EEC	European Economic Community
EFIM	Agency for the Central Control and Finance of Manufacturing Industry
EMA	European Monetary Agreement
EMS	European Monetary System
EMU	European Monetary Union
ENEL	National Agency for Electrical Energy
ENI	National Hydrocarbon Corporation
EPU	European Payments Union
EU	European Union
FED	Federal Reserve Board
FIAT	Italian Factory of Cars in Turin

FIM	Engineering Industry Fund
FOB	Free on Board
GDP	Gross Domestic Product
GKO	Russian Treasury Bills
ICI	Local Property Tax
ICIAP	Local Property Tax on Business Premises
ICS	Institute for Special Credit
ILOR	Local Income Tax
IMF	International Monetary Fund
IMI	Italian Financing Institute
INA	National Insurance Institute
IPI	Company Property Tax
IRAP	Regional Tax on Productive Activities
IRI	Italian Institute for Industrial Reconstruction
IRPEF	Personal Income Tax
IRPEG	Corporation Tax
ISI	Extraordinary Property Tax
ISTAT	Italian Central Statistics Institute
M1	Monetary Aggregate
M2	Monetary Aggregate
M2A	Monetary Aggregate
M3	Monetary Aggregate
NAFTA	North Atlantic Free Trade Agreement
NASDAQ	National Association of Securities Dealers Automated Quotations
OECD	Organization for Economic Co-operation and Development
OEEC	Organization for European Economic Co-operation
OPEC	Organization of Petroleum Exporting Countries
PA	Public Administration
PMI	Small and Medium Sized Enterprises
STET	Turin Telephone Company
TDC	Total Domestic Credit
UIC	Foreign Exchange Authority
UIL	Italian Trade Unions Confederation
VAT	Value Added Tax

1. The Italian Economy in the Immediate Post-War Period

> *Progressive capitalist economies expand [...] thanks to the combined effect of population growth, technical progress in production and the general public's propensity to save; and thanks to the intervention of enterprises. The first three factors create the necessary conditions for new investments, which are essential for the expansion of the economy, to take place; that is, they determine the extent and rhythm of the* potential expansion *of investments. Enterprises transform the latter into* actual expansion, *by making the new investments which gradually become sufficiently profitable, thanks to the potential expansion.* (Fanno, 1956, p. 353).

1.1 Problems of reconversion and reconstruction

After the Second World War, which virtually devastated the countries engaged in conflict, vigorous measures to transform the war economies back into peacetime economies were required. This was a momentous and arduous task: the experience of the previous post-war period and the bitter memories of the 1929 Crisis sparked fears of a return to overproduction and unemployment in the non-communist countries. This is why policy objectives focused principally upon the achievement of full employment.

A crucial consequence of the Second World War was the division of the world into two spheres of influence, with the Union of Soviet Socialist Republics on one side and the United States of America on the other blocs upon which; the nations tied to the two powers came to depend upon these blocs. Fundamental issues such as war debts, financial reserves and monetary convertibility emerged and were to dominate the international economic scene for many years to come.

At the end of the Second World War Italy was faced with three types of problem: reconversion of industry, reconstruction of war damage, and deep-rooted problems of a structural nature. The most pressing structural problem was the level of unemployment. This was evidently linked to the business cycle,[1] which in turn was related to the events of the war; it was also related to structural elements in the Italian economy. The rate of income growth was never sufficient to absorb the natural increase in population, and emigration had become an outlet for excessive population growth. Agriculture had suffered under autarkic fascist policies which focused almost exclusively on the production of cereals, sacrificing livestock and fodder farming. The unmanageable situation in the *Mezzogiorno*, a typically Italian problem[2] and a long-standing feature of the country's history, came to the forefront after 1945.

Undoubtedly the repercussions of reconstruction and reconversion were felt most heavily in industry: initial estimates reported 30% to 40% destruction of output capacity, although in more reliable estimates this figure fell to 8-9% (Graziani, 1972, p. 291). In the light of this fresh evidence, effective damage to industrial equipment was actually rather more limited. In fact,

> the flow of investments did not cease until 1943, since even during the war years, industrial investment programmes planned before Italy joined the war were completed, with a view to resuming production at the end of hostilities. As a result, in 1945, despite war damage, output capacity was one and a half times higher than in 1938. (Gualerni, 1980, p. 24)

Nevertheless the difficulties facing industry were huge. At the time food, textiles and electrical energy were the most important sectors of Italian secondary manufacturing industry.[3] Only the textile industry

---

[1] The initial and certainly partial absorption of female labour was merely a substitute for scarce male labour, deployed on the war front. This brings back to mind the Marxian concept of a reserve industrial army.

[2] Today we still refer to the Southern issue, the North-South gap, the Italian case, or economic dualism, to identify one of the current economy's greatest problems. These terms refer to the gap between an advanced North and a backward South. This vast and complex problem has inspired numerous contributions from home and abroad. The analysis by Trigilia (1992) is undoubtedly of great interest, and investigates distortions produced by state intervention in the *Mezzogiorno*. For a foregoing analysis see Podbielski (1974).

[3] The iron and steel, chemical and car industries in particular were impaired. The country yearned for renovation, and a different structure for the secondary manufacturing sector was proposed. Catholic economists including Vito (1946),

emerged from the war in a favourable state, the other two sectors being substantially incapable of resuming output. The Italian textile industry enjoyed a competitive edge in international markets, and this was safeguarded by the high cost of freight which hindered British competition. Textiles from South-East Asia (India and Japan) were not to appear on world markets for many years to come. In Italy the persistence of priorities typically associated with rural life, such as a taste for fine clothes, helps to explain why the fashion industry flourished.

The shortage of imports slowed down reconstruction efforts, undertaken principally by private individuals and financed by foreign aid. At the same time the sluggish pace of reconstruction undermined the recovery of exports. The result was a vicious circle, the negative impact of which was felt by the entire economic system.

1.2 The peculiarities of the inflationary process

It is hardly surprisingly that the war years were marked by repressed inflation. The Government soaked up liquidity from the private sector and transferred it to the public sector, thereby deflating private demand and dampening inflationary pressure. Banks were invited or compelled to invest liquid funds in the purchase of government bonds rather than by offering private loans. In this way the public sector obtained the liquidity it required without boosting private demand. This was essentially a monetary manoeuvre, enforced to transfer funds from the private to the public sector: private demand was squeezed in favour of public expenditure.

Inflation surged upwards in 1944 and from 1943 to 1945 the uncontrolled printing of banknotes[4] provided a clearly monetary impulse to

---

an expert on trusts, expressed perplexity over the industrialist system, and spoke in no uncertain terms of nationalization. He highlighted of the need to construct an alternative mechanism to the free-market economy, cf. Barucci (1969). The neo-liberal line prevailed, based on the ideology of Einaudi, expounded in his volume «*Lezioni di politica sociale*» (1949). For a general view of the Italian economy in the post-war period see Bresciani Turroni (1957).
In the immediate post-war period, it emerged from a series of debates and conferences that for historical reasons the introduction of full economic planning was impossible. The contribution of Saraceno was decisive in establishing a system of planning which both helped to orient the private economy and was binding for the state economy. Cf. Avagliano (1980).

[4] Thus the type of inflation described by Manoussos (1962, p. 7 onwards) reappeared, the result of «*une augmentation abusive de la quantité de papier-*

inflation. The so-called Allied Military Currency issued by the Allied Government to finance the occupying forces' expenditure[5] bloated the supply of money in circulation. Indeed,

> In contrast to 19 lire to the dollar before the war, the exchange rate fixed imperiously and with no reasonable justification other than to punish a defeated country, was 100 lire to the dollar. (Colajanni, 1990, p. 34)

The result was an appreciable increase in the price of imports, vital for the country's survival. At the same time the purchasing power of the occupying forces increased significantly. However

> given the inflation differential to Italy's disadvantage, the lira was undervalued for a very short time; in fact when the Allied Forces entered Rome, it was overvalued once more. (Spinelli and Fratianni, 1991, p. 416)

Later an opportunity arose to exchange the Allied Military Currency for pounds sterling and dollars, thus it became possible to cope with import requirements at least. Owing to the scarcity of supply, the Italian Government was inclined to abolish all forms of control in the goods market.[6] This led to rapid price increases, and triggered a price-wage spiral

---

monnaie». For an analysis of different types of inflation, see Heertje and Nardi Spiller (1986, Ch. 12).
Today the issue of money no longer constitutes a significant source of resources for the public sector, as it was in the past. Nevertheless a similar situation was observed in the 1970s and 1980s in Argentina, Brazil and other Latin American countries.

[5] The Allied Military Currency so called AM-lire was denominated in notes from 1 to 1,000 lire, and supplemented the 181,235 notes and coins in circulation issued by the State.

[6] In Italy controlled prices were imposed in 1944. In the same year the state imposed price of bread was abolished. The term «controlled prices» may also refer to monopolistic or oligopolistic firms: in this case the appropriate term is «managed prices».
In a regime of controlled prices the maximum price of a good or service is fixed, and can only be modified by the government. Such measures may be permanent (and apply only to the products of monopolistic or oligopolistic firms) or short-lived in an attempt to restrain inflationary pressure. The short-term measures apply to numerous goods and services, in considerable quantities. These measures are considered ineffective since they generate substantial inflationary expectations, so their application should be limited to the short term. In Italy a special case was recorded from July 1973 to 1974. Controlled prices had been in

which took inflation to dramatically[7] high levels.

> [In 1944] the state deficit increased in proportion to income compared to 1943, and so did the portion of the deficit financed by creating monetary base; no medium-term government debt was issued. Overall, there was a slow-down in the rate expansion of the monetary base. However since the multiplier accelerated sharply, monetary growth was practically equal to the 1943 level. Output continued to fall. The rate of inflation peaked during the period. Economic policy consisted solely of fiscal measures, which were bound to increase the state deficit. (Spinelli and Fratianni, 1991, p. 418)

---

force since the post-war period for foodstuffs (bread and milk) and since 1974 for fertilisers and cement, and were lifted in the first half of August 1993 following the CIPE (Interdepartmental Committee for Economic Planning) decree conforming to European Economic Community (EEC) directives. This also resulted in the liberalisation of meat prices. In addition controlled prices were applied to kerosene, diesel oil, school textbooks, cold meats and salamis, etc., and from 1 August 1991 to petrol also. The system of controlled prices imposed a permanent obligation upon the producers of given products and services to provide information on their prices. On 30 September 1993 the CIPE decided to liberalise the prices of petrol products with effect from 1 May 1994. Up to that date the oil companies were obliged to deposit their price lists at the *Ministero dell'Industria* (Ministry of Industry). Later the possibility of agreed prices rather than controlled prices was discussed. In Italy, as in France, Belgium and Holland, the agreement between firms and the State concerned not so much the price level of goods and services but rather the rules that were to be followed for a given period of time.
Prices and/or public tariffs for public services (telephones, electricity, postal services, rail transport, third party liability insurance for motorists) were determined unilaterally by the Public Administration at its discretion.
Price control was exercised by the *Comitato Interministeriale dei Prezzi* (CIP, Interdepartmental Committee on Prices), on the basis of directives received from the CIPE. Price increases requested by manufacturers were authorised by the CIP following a series of investigations to establish that production costs had increased. The CIPE replaced the CIP in 1994.

[7] Inflation resulting from wars or revolutions is often catastrophic, and deprives money of its function. Bresciani Turroni (1931) constitutes a milestone in the study of the German experience, and this analysis was later broadened into a more general vision (1978). Subsequently a version of hyperinflation, defined as inflation equal to or above a monthly rate of 50%, was provided by Cagan (1956), who established that when inflation rises radical changes occur in real balances.

In 1945, the state deficit fell in relation to national income. The monetary situation also improved slightly, in view of the *Prestito della Liberazione* (Five Year Liberation Loan),[8] and, somewhat surprisingly in this case, the inflation rate dropped sharply. Although this fall in inflation could to a limited extent be explained by a marginal recovery in aggregate supply, the main explanation was the decisive role played by expectations. A widespread sentiment of better times to come, persuaded individuals to refrain from spending, with a positive impact on prices. Hopes were dashed in 1946 when inflation surged upwards once more. The loss of confidence lowered expectations, and monetary pressure intensified.[9]

This distressing state of affairs caused serious economic and social problems. The reorganisation of production processes and distribution systems led to the redistribution of income in favour of the trading classes. A dual proposal was put forward in an attempt to resolve this situation. On the one hand, it was asserted that controls over the goods market were necessary (the rationing of consumer goods), while on the other a currency reform was propounded as a way to absorb liquidity from the private sector. Thus rationing and currency reform became the central themes of heated debate.

The currency reform was supported by the left wing, as a way to restore the monetary balance and to tax excess profits derived from speculation. The right wing argued that such a measure would have negative repercussions on the savings of the middle classes, which up to that moment had subscribed the public loans. The introduction of the new currency was thwarted when the Bank of Italy announced that the country lacked the necessary security to safely distribute and introduce the new currency.[10]

---

[8] The *Prestito della Liberazione*, advocated by the Treasury Minister Marcello Soleri in May 1945 raised 106 billion lire, through the issue of 5 year bonds with an interest rate of 5%.

[9] Between 1946 and 1947 the state deficit was financed at least in part by the 5 year the *Prestito della Ricostruzione* (Reconstruction Loan) proposed by the Treasury Minister Giovanni Battista Bertone, which created an inferior quantity of monetary base. The loan was financed by 30 year bonds, and an exemption clause excluded the bonds from any form extraordinary taxation subsequently levied. The initial rate of interest was 3.5%, subsequently rising to 5%. The loan raised 231 billion lire.

[10] The currency changeover was abandoned upon discovery of the theft of copies of the matrix to be used for printing the new notes. The suggestion that the project was shelved for these reasons appears unconvincing. On this subject cf. Spinelli and Fratianni (1991, p. 418, n. 30). On the most important aspects of the currency changeover controversy at the time, see Dell'Orefice (1985).

Intervention in the goods market was obstructed by those who ruled out all forms of control, reflecting their ardent desire to distance themselves from the Fascist regime and the corporate system by refusing a managed economy. Indeed the most pressing requirement was to dismantle the political structure of the authoritarian state, and with it any residual elements of the corporate system, and to return to a competitive economy based on private enterprise. It was not feared that liberal economic policies might lead to inflation, since public spending was firmly believed to be the principal source of inflation. The private and banking sectors were certainly not considered capable of undermining monetary stability.

Economic policy focused on the abolition of all forms of price control; banks were free to finance the economy, inevitably aggravating inflation. The scarcity of consumer goods pushed prices up and in turn this led to wage rises. Producers retaliated with further price increases (sparking profit inflation), and as a result the demand for liquidity rose in monetary terms at least. In such conditions banks were eager to finance enterprise, and in doing so further increased liquidity. By generating a climate of mistrust, inflation accelerated the velocity of circulation; rocketing prices rises triggered speculation both in the goods and securities markets.

The Government remained firmly convinced that public expenditure was the only source of inflation and reduced expenditure on reconstruction, doing nothing however to limit the expansion of credit, in fact a key factor in the development of inflation.

1.3 An analysis of anti-inflationary measures

Reconstruction and reconversion proceeded in a climate of tension, despite a slowdown in the rate of inflation recorded in 1945, mainly to be attributed to the role of expectations. A common spirit of renewal pervaded the country and Italians pinned their hopes on the United States: much was expected of the American people, and in this mood, demand contracted. It is interesting to note the analogy with the events of 1918-1919:

> the similarity between the two historical periods appears to be even greater if we observe that in both cases, at the end of hostilities, following an initial fall, inflation rebounded sharply. After the Second World War, the increase was between the spring of 1946 and that of 1947. (Spinelli and Fratianni, 1991, p. 420)

The inflationary impulse recorded between June 1946 and September 1947 was the result of growth in demand for investment and consumer goods over and above the limited resources available. Lively debate ensued over appropriate policy measures: potential strategies included measures to deflate internal demand, provided that this led to a fall in investment, or alternatively the devaluation of the lira.[11]

In terms of exchange rate policies, it is important to consider the fundamental importance of critical elasticities.[12] It is immediately apparent

[11] The terms devaluation and revaluation are more appropriate in a fixed exchange rate system, while depreciation and appreciation are used in a floating exchange rate system. However this distinction is often overlooked. In fixed exchange systems, devaluation increases the exchange rate. In this case, we obtain: internal currency (variable)/foreign currency (fixed). In a system of floating exchange rates, we obtain: foreign currency (variable)/internal currency (fixed), i.e. the opposite. Most countries opted for fixed exchange rates, with the exception of Great Britain (which excluded currencies such as the Indian rupee and the Arab riyal from the system), the United States (which excluded the pound sterling and exchange rates on banknotes from all other countries from the system), and certain countries in South-East Asia such as Thailand and Hong Kong. On this cf. Astolfi and Negri (1993, p. 565). Currently countries within the Euro-area operate fixed exchange rates between their currencies.

[12] If we define export elasticity (ε_E) and import elasticity (ε_M) with respect to the exchange rate as each price elasticity, i.e. as a relationship between the proportional variation in the quantity and the proportional variation in the price (denoted in this case by the exchange rate: r). Where E denotes exports and M denotes imports, we obtain:

$$\varepsilon_E = \frac{\Delta E / E}{\Delta r / r} \quad e \quad \varepsilon_M = \frac{\Delta M / M}{\Delta r / r}$$

The necessary condition for an improvement in the balance of payments is clearly that the increased value of exports exceeds the increased value of imports. Given that p_E and p_M represent export prices and import prices (expressed in a single foreign currency of reference) we obtain:

$$\varepsilon_E p_E E > (1 - \varepsilon_M) r p_M M, \qquad [1.1]$$

and by dividing both sides by $rp_M M$ and reorganising the equation, we arrive at:

$$\frac{p_E E}{r p_M M} \varepsilon_E + \varepsilon_M > 1 \qquad [1.2]$$

With an initial balance of payments equilibrium so that $p_E E = rp_M M$, [1.2] becomes:

that a devaluation improves[13] a deficit in so far as it stimulates exports while imports become more expensive. However it is important not to overlook the fact that the growth of exports generates a corresponding

$$\varepsilon_E + \varepsilon_M > 1 \qquad [1.3]$$

i.e. the sum of export elasticity and import elasticity (in absolute terms) must be greater than 1 in order for a currency devaluation to improve the balance of payments.
[1.3] is known as the Marshall-Lerner condition, although there is some doubt over Marshall's involvement (Gandolfo, 1986, p. 109). See also Marshall (1961). An essay by Bickerdicke (1920) and a later essay by Joan Robinson (1950) seem to precede Lerner (1944) in terms of the formal, correct definition of exchange rate stability. Perhaps a more appropriate term might be the Bickerdicke-Robinson condition. In this context Gandolfo underlined that «It would be even better to abandon all reference to persons and use an objective definition such as for example "critical elasticities condition"» (Gandolfo, 1986, Vol. II, p. 109. Ciravegna (1997, pp. 244-55) also entered the controversy expressly emphasising from an analytical standpoint the motivations behind the two distinct terms. Indeed in his approach Bickerdike's condition of critical elasticities "becomes" the Marshall-Lerner condition when from an initial state of equilibrium in the balance of payments, we hypothesise infinite elasticity of supply of imported and exported goods (*Ibid.*, p. 249).
To identify the condition in which net outlays fall or net receipts rise in foreign currency, we can turn to the balance of payments expressed in foreign currency. Given that $B = p_E E - r_{pM} M$ represents the balance of payments in internal currency and $B' = 1/r\ p_E E - r_{pM} M$ that in foreign currency, in the initial case of equilibrium in the balance of payments the condition remains [1.3], while in the case of disequilibrium in the balance of payments, we obtain:

$$\varepsilon_E + \frac{rp_M M}{p_E E}\varepsilon_M > 1 \qquad [1.4]$$

13 If we focus on devaluation of the exchange rate in a fixed exchange rate system, let us suppose in this context that the critical elasticity condition has been fulfilled. Consequently the money supply tends to increase, leading to a shift in the monetary equilibrium curve, which persists as long as there is a balance of payments surplus. However devaluation, which boosts internal consumption and accentuates the shift in the real equilibrium curve, may lead to an increase in the general price level. As a result nominal demand for money grows, so that graphically the monetary equilibrium curve would shift to the left.

increase in internal demand.[14]

Within the sphere of decision making, policy choices must also take the level of employment into account. In 1946 policy makers considered Italy to be in a state of full employment and consequently chose to remain "actively" absent, a somewhat controversial opinion. They justified their decision on the grounds that although widespread unemployment existed in the labour market, fixed capital was fully employed, creating considerable bottlenecks in the economy. Thus it was unavoidably necessary to deflate aggregate demand, rather than to reduce the propensity to import.

The fall in aggregate demand was achieved by monetary action to restrict credit circulation,[15] so that

> The 1947 measures after often singled out as a classic example of how to bring an inflationary spiral to an abrupt halt by appropriate control of the level of credit. One of the most significant and distinctive effects of these measures was renewed saving. (Bresciani Turroni, 1957, p. 11)

The inflationary spiral was halted, but with tangible effects on the real economy: firms became short of liquidity, the pace of activity slowed and industrial investment declined, with counterproductive effects which delayed the process of reconstruction.

The outbreak of the Korean War (June 1950) was decisive, not only in terms of the distressing conflict which involved several countries, but it also in terms of its theoretical and practical implications: the Korean War emphasised the fundamental role of imported inflation. In the United States this triggered a peculiar type of inflation, induced by demand shifting between sectors (Schultze, 1959). On the other hand, Italy benefited from the increase in price levels in international markets: Italian prices became relatively more competitive and exports grew substantially.

---

[14] In this context the induced volume of imports is crucial in so far as it has a virtual feedback effect. In a two country model, if country A increases its imports from country B, the exports and income of the latter increase. However the higher level of income leads to a higher level of imports. Thus a change in the level of imports of country A has a feedback effect on its exports.

[15] On 4 August 1947, the *Comitato Interministeriale per il Credito e il Risparmio* (CICR, Interdepartmental Committee on Credit and Saving) met for the first time under chairman Luigi Einaudi, and later issued the directive implementing the credit squeeze. Between October and December 1947, the new regulations on the reserve requirement came into effect.

1.4 The specific role of the exchange rate

The unfaltering will to oppose previous economic policies, and to dissociate with fascist protectionism prompted the principal economies to vigorously support free trade.

In Italy the textile sector was in a favourable condition, but nevertheless its requirements of raw materials and machinery called for an adequate capacity to import. Precise measures were required to ensure that sufficient import licences were granted. However the government, in seeking to distance itself from the former regime, strongly opposed any form of control. Entrepreneurs in the textile industry pressed for liberalisation of foreign exchange, in order to use export revenues in foreign markets, free from all forms of taxation, instead of surrendering their foreign exchange to the *Ufficio Italiano Cambi* (UIC, Foreign Exchange Authority) and procuring an import licence on each occasion.

It should be remembered that at the time Italy was in the process of joining the Western bloc, and that the United States were striving to achieve ever closer integration between European states. It is easy to appreciate why our policy makers were compelled by internal and external influences to adopt free trade policies.

In 1946 pressure from exporters were such that the dollar was revalued from 100 to 225 lire.[16] At the end of March 50% of export income was liberalised, while the remaining 50% had to be surrendered at official prices to the UIC. This led to the creation of a free market with higher exchange rates come to exist alongside the official controlled foreign exchange market, effectively constituting a devaluation of the lira.

Although this state of affairs increased profits for exporters, it did nothing to improve the balance of payments: demand for Italian exports was rigid, and devaluation could not increase foreign demand significantly. Many were of the opinion that it would have been more appropriate to focus on efforts on exchange controls, thereby limiting the capacity to import of the export sectors. However such controls did not tally with government policies and exchange rates were liberalised; in 1949, the dollar was worth 625 lire.

It is vital to remember that most European countries were also enduring alarming monetary and financial hardship:[17] their most urgent needs could

[16] The extra 125 lire were used as an export premium.

[17] The end of war hostilities called for redefinition of the monetary situation, which was accomplished with the Bretton Woods Agreement. The White Plan (7 April 1943) aimed to extend the gold exchange standard (whereby internal currencies were convertible into foreign currency and in turn into gold), to the

not be covered by severely depleted gold reserves, and their currencies were virtually worthless. The United States was the only nation in a position to provide what was necessary, and thus a desperate rush to procure dollars ensued. The «thirst for dollars» led in 1958 to complete freedom to change any currency into dollars, and from dollars potentially into gold.

1.5 The gradual adoption of Keynesian prescriptions

During the fascist years, economic policies were corporative,[18] characterised by strong State intervention in an economy which ultimately became protectionist and autarchic. The subsequent reaction to this type of regime heralded a return to liberalistic ideas, and to the growing conviction that

> free markets solve numerous problems which all the wisdom of the law cannot solve. (Del Vecchio, 1950, p. 397)

This liberalistic inspiration acted as a stimulus to numerous power centres, namely the Issuing Institute, the *Ministero del Bilancio* (Ministry for the Budget, specially established for Luigi Einaudi), the *Ministero del Commercio con l'Estero* (the Ministry of Foreign Trade) and the UIC. The right to strike and the revival of free trade unions both contributed to the dismantling of the previous institutional framework. At the same time

---

advantage of the dollar. In such a regime, the reserves of the issuing bank could consist of currencies which were convertible into gold, in particular pounds sterling and dollars. The Keynes Plan (8 April 1943) was more universal, in the sense that all issuing banks were to deposit their gold reserves in a world bank which would in turn issue an international currency, the *bancor*, with which to finance deficit countries. The solutions adopted at Bretton Woods (July 1944) were closer to the White Plan than to the Keynes's Plan.
Triffin (1947; 1961) drew attention to the inherent contradiction in the Bretton Woods system of fixed exchange rates in relation to the dollar. In fact on the one hand a US balance of payments deficit became necessary to increase world liquidity, on the other hand persistent deficits undermined confidence in the dollar. Thus we see that if we maintain constant the gold content of the reserve currency, the system risks providing insufficient international liquidity; conversely if this function is abandoned, there is the risk that the gold content of the reserve currency will not be maintained.

[18] For a clear comparison between the corporative (fascist) model and the non-corporative (social-democratic) model, see Valli (1990, p. 265).

there was a gradual opening on the foreign policy front, as Italy became a member of the numerous international organisations which strove to foster increasing interdependency between states in the name of ever greater liberalisation of trade.

The diverse strategic and speculative approach which evolved[19] in Italy yielded a surprising result: the implementation of a middle-class policy which radically contrasted with the staunch participation of the working classes in the nation's civilian recovery. The result was

> the constant shelving of "economic reforms", which were merely paid lip service. (Caffè, 1984, p. 382)

Nevertheless State intervention in the Italy's economic life showed no signs of retracting. IRI (the Italian Institute for Industrial Reconstruction), AGIP (the Italian Petroleum Company) and IMI (the Italian Financing Institute) continued to exist, and the role of state-sector companies certainly did not diminish.

Keynes's ideas gained ground in the 1950's, in terms both of their conceptual relevance and their practical applications, although the same ideas were harshly criticised in the subsequent decade.[20] Keynes's theories by no means gained immediate support,[21] indeed it was hard not to succumb to the intellectual charm of liberalism; clashes between liberalistic and Keynesian stances[22] were frequent. The conflict had already

---

[19] For an analysis of speculative approaches and policies in Italy up to the end of the 1979's, cf. Lunghini (1981).

[20] Monetarism *à la* Friedman and later the New Classical Economics led Keynesian prescriptions to be set aside. See the classical authors Friedman and Schwartz (1963; 1965); Lucas (1973; 1981; 1987) and Lucas and Sargent (1981).

[21] In the early 1930s there was lively debate surrounding the controversy between von Hayek and Keynes. In Italy economists subscribed to the theory of over-investment, thus signalling the supremacy of von Hayek's theory over Keynes's theory, and revealing Italian opposition to Keynesian principles before the publication of the *General Theory*. In Italian academic circles, Fanno (1956) endeavoured to provide a synthesis of the two separate approaches. On this see Nardi Spiller (1993; 2000a) and Magliulo (1998). For a more general view of Keynes's influence in Italy, see Bini and Magliulo (1997).

[22] In the 1960s Keynesian style economic policies were fully accepted by Britain and the United States, indeed an analytical and operative framework emerged: the so-called New Economics. See Heller (1967). This approach stressed the overriding objective of restoring full employment in the wake of the high levels of unemployment recorded during the 1950s, and emphasised the importance of

surfaced during the debate on the 1947 credit squeeze and was accentuated by discussions of a programme of public investment funded by the Marshall Plan[23] aimed at reducing the high rate of unemployment.

---

the monetary wage trend in relation to variations in productivity as a factor influencing the rate of inflation. Thus monetary wages were not to increase faster than the average rate of productivity growth in the economy, which was given by the ratio of labour input to output.

[23] The Marshall Plan was implemented immediately after the end of the Second World War. After the 1990 Gulf War its re-introduction was proposed for certain Arab nations, and once again in 2001 for certain countries devastated by war or recession. On behalf of the United States General Marshall put forward a plan of aid for the European economies, and this plan took his name. The proposals were innovative in so far as they introduced the concept of the economics of aid. The Marshall Plan was undoubtedly the driving force behind the renewed economic activity and monetary reorganisation in the European states after the war.

There was a marked change in US policy towards Western Europe, from a relatively passive approach towards direct intervention, culminating on 5 June 1947 with the Secretary of State George Marshall's speech at Harvard University. The aim was to create a pro-US bloc in the Western world. The Soviet authorities denounced the "imperialist" nature of the initiative, and forced the Eastern European countries (Poland and above all Czechoslovakia) which were initially open towards the US, to categorically refuse the programme. The start of the European Recovery Programme, which involved sixteen European nations and the three western zones of Germany, was launched in April 1948. In Italy however concerns expressed by the Liberal School, anxious to defend the value of the lira, became so great that its representatives in the Government refused a part of the aid, for fear of rekindling inflation. They were harshly criticised by the United States.

A centralised organisation, the Economic Co-operation Administration was established and the European nations purchased raw materials and machinery from all over the world with dollars supplied by the US Government: member states effectively received their share of goods free of charge. They then sold the machinery or processed raw materials in the internal market in exchange for internal currency. This counter-value was administered by the central banks and could be employed to fund public works or repay loans. This system was of considerable importance in terms of monetary policy: by using the counter-value of the Marshall Plan to extinguish debts or to fund public works normally financed from the state budget, state finances improved, value was restored to internal currencies and possible sources of inflation were reduced. One of the merits of the Marshall Plan, which was due to end in 1952 but actually continued until the 1960s, was that it compelled European nations to co-operate with each other on an ongoing basis in the field of economic policy. The Organisation for European Economic Co-operation (OEEC) was established up

However the foundation of the *Cassa del Mezzogiorno*[24] in 1950 (with law 646 of 10 August) brought one of liberalism's greatest limits to the fore: the inability of the free market to redress the marked and long-standing imbalance deriving from the North-South gap.[25]

for the purpose of monetary co-operation, and a series of monetary agreements followed: the European Payments Union (EPU, 17 June 1950) and the European Monetary Agreement (EMA, 27 December 1958). The EMA assured all the necessary clearing operations and made it possible to transfer currencies between European countries. The agreement made currencies convertible and thus the gold exchange standard came into effect.

[24] The *Cassa del Mezzogiorno* was a government agency with responsibility for planning, funding and implementing works to promote social and economic progress in the South of Italy. Initially endowed with 100 billion lire, the agency was subsequently assigned additional funds on several occasions and continued to exist until 1984, when it was wound up. In 1986 the *Agenzia per la Promozione dello Sviluppo nel Mezzogiorno* (APSM, Agency for the Promotion and Development of the *Mezzogiorno*) was established, which ceased to exist on 15 April 1993. For a detailed examination of the role of state intervention in the South of Italy, see among others, Bodo and Sestito (1991).

[25] Every nation experienced, to a greater or lesser extent and in its own peculiar way, the phenomenon of dualism, which was however unique in Italy's case. The reunification of Germany aroused interest once again in such issues and stimulated new studies. See Pizzini and Nardi Spiller (2003).

2. The Great Leap and the Subsequent U-Turn

The "Italian crisis" was not merely an economic crisis. It eluded those who examined the events of these years from a purely macroeconomic perspective. Yet it evolved gradually, first and foremost as a consequence of the imbalances created by the "miracle" and the incapacity of political and economic figures to deal with the problems old and new emerging or re-emerging during the phase of development which began in the early 1960s. (Lombardini, 1974, p. 5)

2.1 The years of the economic miracle

The Marshall Plan undoubtedly afforded a tangible contribution to development in European countries and at the same time acted as a catalyst for integration and European union, prompting the foundation of the first common organisations for a better use of aid.[1] However we must not

[1] On 22 September 1947 the Committee of European Economic Co-operation, established two months previously to organise the use of Marshall Plan funds approved a report advocating a system of economic union between nations, and the application of a multilateral clearing system for foreign trade. On 18 November France, Italy, Belgium, The Netherlands and Luxembourg, as permanent members - later joined by Germany - signed a multilateral European monetary clearing agreement. The process of integration gathered pace and led on 18 April 1951 to the foundation of the European Coal and Steel Community (ECSC) and in March 1957 to the establishment of the EEC. The agreement provided for the creation of a customs union by means of the gradual abolition of all public tariffs on foreign trade between member states. Rules and principles were established to prevent discrimination and restriction of competition. Full convertibility of currencies was achieved in 1958, heralding the end of the EPU.

overlook the explanation provided by the vintage models[2] which appropriately interpret the astounding levels of growth witnessed in the post-war period by Italy, Germany and Japan, three nations harshly hit by the Second World War.

As circumstances evolved, Italy began to record an increasingly encouraging trade balance, the decline in imports gradually being counterbalanced by export growth. Italy surmounted its traditional definition of a closed economy, developing into an open economy as foreign trade became ever more important. Exports played a preponderant role in the transition process and became vital for economic growth, boosting national income substantially. Greater balance was achieved in the state budget; and budget and monetary policy were integrated, although a clear distinction persisted between the Treasury and the Bank of Italy, the latter maintaining a considerable degree of autonomy. Remarkable success was achieved:

> The portion of government expenditure financed by the deficit decreased steadily, from 31.6% of expenditure in the financial year 1949-50 to 22.1% in 1954-55. At the same time government revenues doubled, and the ratio between the state deficit and gross domestic product remained constant at around 0.5%.The structure of public spending also became more stable at last: the level of extraordinary expenditure, which in 1948-49 was still 50% of total expenditure, plummeted to 5% in 1954-55. (Colajanni, 1990, p. 80)

The deflationary use of Marshall Plan transfers was conducive to the achievement of these encouraging results. The counter-value in lire of US credits was detained in state coffers for as long as possible to fulfil the Treasury's funding requirements. Monetary policy was not apparently focused on stimulating internal growth, despite intervention to regulate liquidity and thereby assure the correct working of the real economy. The result was a low inflation rate and limited growth in money circulation.

---

[2] This expression denotes economic growth models in which capital is not considered homogeneous but rather a series of past investments, each with unique characteristics and a different level of technology with respect its predecessor. The theory that the high growth rate during the post-war period was the result of the reconstruction of capital stock was disputed in the case of Japan. On this cf. Christiano (1989) and Hayashi (1989).
In reality when countries experience war or revolution, they consider whether or not it is appropriate to rationalise the economy: the drastic reduction in capital stock calls for substitution, and investments with a higher technological content. See Olsen (1982). Certainly a similar possibility emerges from Solow's model. See Solow (1956).

Credit expanded without fuelling inflationary pressure and financed the economy, which led to considerable capital accumulation in view of the limited state borrowing requirement.[3]

Growth in output was striking[4] between 1948 and 1955, and at the same time profound structural changes were observed. In this context,

> large firms were the driving force behind the rapid recovery [...] in this way large firms propagated entrepreneurship. The diffusion of entrepreneurship was however closely tied to large-scale enterprise. Its concentration in the North served only to accentuate the gap with the *Mezzogiorno*. (Colajanni, 1990, p. 82)

The years from 1951 to 1961, or some would say more appropriately from 1958[5] to 1961, are generally labelled the «boom years» or the «years of the economic miracle».[6] Three features distinguish this period:

a) the rate of capital accumulation, i.e. the share of national income dedicated to investment, which reached astonishing levels;

b) the general price level which gave no cause for concern: even though prices were increasing at a rate of 3-4%; far from creating problems, this

---

[3] This phenomenon was also favoured the high propensity to save of households.

[4] Policies to promote industrial reconversion were implemented in part by establishing new banks which offered medium and long term credit, in addition to the existing banks. *Mediobanca* was founded in 1946. The engineering industry was financed directly by the Government through the *Fondo per le Industrie Meccaniche* (FIM) (Engineering Industry Fund). Later, when the credits became uncollectable and were transformed into shareholdings, the latter became a management agency, the *Ente Partecipazione e Finanza Industria Manifatturiera* (EFIM) (Agency for the Central Control and Finance of Manufacturing Industry). The public role was crucial for the Italian industrialization, see Cohen and Federico (2001).

[5] We recall that in 1958 the lira won an award as the most stable currency.

[6] On the anniversary of the Unification of Italy, it emerged (Banca d'Italia, *Relazione Economica*, 1961) that per capita real income had tripled between 1861 to 1969, although more than half of this increase was achieved in the comparatively short period between 1951 and 1960. Later it became clear (in a footnote presented on 22 May 1962 to Parliament by the Treasury Minister) that despite the Italian economy's growth potential, national economic development could not be considered an automatic process: development could not proceed automatically without its repercussions being felt by the entire economy. Certain needs also surfaced gradually, essentially consisting in the necessary «conditions for an orderly and free society» (Léon, 1979, p. 310).

modest increase boosted production;[7]

c) balance of payments stability.

The predominant features of this phase of development witnessed throughout the entire country[8] were the extremely brisk export trend and the moderate wage trend determined by the excess supply of labour, which weakened trade union power. Evidence of this emerges clearly from a comparison of productivity and wage trends. If we take 1953 as the base year equal to 100, the productivity index reached 184 in 1961, whereas the wage index stood at 147 (Graziani, 1972, pp. 303-4).

Changes in the distribution of income had significant consequences, with a gradual decrease in the proportion of income derived from subordinate employment up to 1961. The low propensity to consume in turn produced a low multiplier, so that potential increases in income were limited and monetary equilibrium was not subject to destabilising forces.

Wage rises below the rate of productivity growth favoured an upward profit trend, which provided finance for investment. This self-financing removed a substantial part of financial flows from the reach of monetary authorities, but also enabled the numerous distortions of the relatively new financial markets to be overcome.

2.2 The structure of the money supply and financial markets

The Italian financial structure at the time was extremely straightforward, the key players being the issuing bank, the lending banks and the Treasury. During the years of the «economic miracle» banks were restricted in their choice of lending: liquid funds were placed either in the private sector or in

[7] In this context, there was a firm conviction that a low level of inflation could drive the economy. The inflation-development relationship became a subject of debate particularly in the 1960s. It was argued that production could be sustained by a reasonable degree of price change. See the pioneering essays on this theme by Kaldor (1959) and Rostow (1959; 1960).

[8] It should be noted that at the peak of its growth, the Italian economy could reach a state of full employment only in so far we can speak of full employment in a dualistic economic system, with overemployment in the North and underemployment in the South.
There was a noticeable shift in emphasis in terms of capital accumulation. The policy of investing in agriculture and infrastructures was abandoned, and attention focused exclusively on industrialisation. This led to the first laws offering incentives and more stringent policies to increase state control in enterprises up to 60% of total investment. However the industrialisation of the *Mezzogiorno* resulted in a decline in the level of employment given the capital intensive nature of investment and the scarcity of skilled labour.

government bonds. Following policies to stabilise yields on the government debt, bonds became risk-free and were widely used within the banking system. Given the lack of alternative lending facilities, the Treasury was compelled to provide banks with sufficient government bonds to soak up all the banks liquidity. Thus up to 1962 the monthly issue of bonds was based not on the liquidity requirements of the Treasury, rather on the liquidity held in the banking sector. The monetary authorities had renounced open market operations[9] as an instrument for regulating liquidity, since the buying and selling of government bonds would have led to fluctuations in yields.

After 1960, Italian banks started to operate on the eurodollar market[10] with the authorisation of the central bank, and later the eurocurrency and

[9] In open market operations the central bank buys and sells bonds in the money markets to regulate the monetary base. The monetary base consists of financial assets which can be used by lending banks as reserves against deposits or which are readily convertible on demand into reserve instruments by the monetary authorities. Such operations are exclusively an instrument of monetary policy since they alter the composition of financial assets and not accumulation (such as a deficit which requires monetary expansion or an increase in bonds). Open market operations may be permanent, if the effect of the variation in the money supply lasts up to maturity; or temporary if at the same time as the purchase (or sale) the central bank sells (or purchases) forward, usually at a few days. In the 1980s these operations became the principal instrument for regulating liquidity within the banking system in most major countries.

[10] Eurodollars were private (non-government) accounts in dollars held at European banks and branches of American banks in Europe. There is no consensus over the motives that led to the creation of such a market. According to some commentators, this was the result of Soviet influence. In fact during the Korean War the Russian authorities shifted their dollar deposits from American to European banks, fearing possible "freezes". However an alternative explanation suggest that it was the London banks which attracted Soviet deposits to London by offering high interest rates, to bypass the credit restrictions on the financing of foreign trade imposed upon the United Kingdom. Cf. Stammati (1975, p. 192). Kindleberger (1969, p. 660) underlines a third aspect. Regulation Q, introduced by the Federal Reserve and abolished in 1980, fixed rates of interest on term deposits but did not apply to term deposits of foreign origin. Such deposits increased significantly between 1958 and 1959, and in order to earn higher profits banks - initially in London and later on the Continent - sought deposits in dollars to re-deposit in New York.
The eurodollar market, which has grown considerably in recent years, made it easier to finance deficits associated with oil imports but undermined anti-inflationary policies and jeopardised the stability of the euromarkets.

external currency markets developed.[11] This led to considerable movements of capital which strengthened the short-term international markets, and to increasing flows between countries. But this also led to the rapid transmission of monetary tension and sizeable speculative operations.

In 1962 it was decided that the monthly bond issue should correspond to the liquidity requirements of the Treasury. In this way the Treasury was guaranteed the funds it required, and at the same time banks were permitted to lend their excess liquid funds in foreign markets.

This coincided with a profound change in the internal structure of the banking system. In the immediate post-war period, the scarcity of postal deposits caused by the proliferation of local banks meant that the role of the *Cassa Depositi e Prestiti*, the credit institute hitherto responsible for financing local authorities had lessened. It became necessary to seek alternative means of financing these agencies, and it was decided was taken to supplement their budgets directly from the state budget. This procedure only rectified the deficits incurred in the relevant accounting period[12] of the local or provincial authorities, so that they were forced to turn to local lending banks to cover their overall borrowing requirements.[13] The authorities soon became some of the best customers of the local banks, since their solvency would sooner or later be guaranteed by the transfer of funds from the state budget. The Italian central bank experienced considerable difficulty in controlling the money supply up to 1962, since up to then reserve requirements[14] could include short-term bonds. This made it possible for the banking system to meet reserve requirements following an expansion of deposits by using such bonds without a reduction in their liquidity.

---

[11] Banks in European countries could accept deposits and make loans in currencies other than the dollar. Similar operations were also performed by non-European banks, so that the term «external currency market» was preferred.

[12] Accrued balances record amounts that the State is liable to pay or entitled to receive, while cash balances record amounts that have actually been paid or received.

[13] This gave rise to a peculiar state of affairs. The smaller banks operating in small towns had difficulty in lending all their liquid funds, while larger banks in industrial centres were unable to attract sufficient liquid funds. The larger banks thus attracted liquid funds from the smaller banks, which in turn opened deposits at the larger banks. Generally the larger banks were controlled by the public sector, while the smaller banks were controlled by private financial groups.

[14] The reserve requirement coefficient varied according to the type of deposit and the type of bank until 1975, when it was unified.

2.3 Inflation in the 1960s

The year 1962 heralded the first reversal in the wage trend: wage increases exceeded productivity growth, favoured by the long-standing process of wage drift.[15] In the face of increasing wages, firms attempted to restore customary profit margins by increasing prices,[16] which in turn led to higher wholesale prices. There was also an alarming change in the balance of payments:[17] imports grew rapidly while export growth diminished.

After ten years of creeping inflation the Italian economy evolved into a state of open inflation. There was specific interest in the interpretation of such a process and two possible explanations were advanced. On the one hand it was suggested that since the country was experiencing wage inflation, the rise in the internal price level had resulted in higher export prices, making Italian products less competitive. In contrast to this clearly entrepreneurial approach was the interpretation offered by the trade unions, who upheld the legitimacy of wage growth, on the grounds that wages had remained below the productivity trend for too long. The trade unions attempted to recover lost time, and accused entrepreneurs of misusing profits accumulated during the economic boom (Graziani, 1972, p. 317), rather than allocating them to improving efficiency.

With all probability both versions contain elements of truth: «*in medio stat virtus*», as the medieval scholastic adage recites. Indeed throughout the economic boom, the Italian economy was heavily reliant upon the trend of overseas demand for consumer goods, and consequently also on

[15] Wage drift occurs in situations of demand inflation. In fact in the well-known equation $D_L = nD_g$, where D_L is labour demand, n is the number of hours necessary to produce a unit of output, D_g represents aggregate demand for goods and services. An increase in the latter leads to an increase in the labour demand. Faced with higher labour demand, firms "hoard" workers, offering extra bonuses and incentives. Wages increase in relation to wage rates. Trade unions only intervene, if at all, at a later stage to obtain an increase in wage rates. See Heertje and Nardi Spiller (1986, p. 314). About the demand-pull and cost push, cf. Lutz (1958).

[16] For a theoretical analysis of wage dynamics and the profit margin trend, see Nardi Spiller (1990b, pp. 71-6).

[17] From 1962-63 the increase in workers' income led to a considerable increase in food consumption, the result being a deficit in the trade balance and a marked increase in prices. On the other hand this exceptionally rapid increase in wages during the two year period was also caused by the increase in agricultural prices, partly due to poor harvests and import restrictions (purchases of livestock products). Cf. Sylos Labini (1982, p. 339, n. 2).

the policies introduced in export markets. The real difficulty that Italy faced was thus its dependence on an external and hence uncontrollable variable, which rendered the country extremely vulnerable.

The consequences of these close ties with overseas markets became apparent in the internal market: the expansion of the export sector was not matched by parallel development in other output sectors dedicated to the internal market, and this

> caused a quantity of labour to abandon agriculture which could not be totally absorbed by industry, given the high intensity of capital investment and the inefficient spread of industry. (Galli and Nannei, 1976, p. 34)

The resulting supply of workers was in part absorbed by the so-called «protected sectors», (non-advanced tertiary sector, Public Administra-tion, construction) which, sheltered from foreign competition, reached huge proportions and earned profits by exploiting conditions of imperfect competition. These sectors passed continuous price rises on to consumers, with modest increases in productivity[18] coupled with wage settlements on a par with the most efficient sector of industry.

In the meantime the Italian institutional framework had evolved significantly. The year 1962 was crucial for the political life of the country as it heralded the opening of the Christian Democrats to the left wing. In November 1963 the Socialist Party entered the government, and this marked the formation of the Centre-Left and in effect ratifying the alliance between two parties, the Christian Democrats and the Italian Socialist Party. This political watershed was accompanied by a number of measures which had profound repercussions upon the financial world (Graziani, 1972, p. 318), namely the nationalization of the electricity companies,[19] the

---

[18] Smith (1975) had already warned of the danger of the expansion of the public sector, diverting resources previously employed in productive occupations towards unproductive occupations. The approach of the New Oxford School, also known as the Old Glasgow School as a tribute to Smith's insight, developed in the United Kingdom inspired principally by Bacon and Eltis (1976). These authors attributed the decline in British growth and the balance of payments problems to the absorption of resources by the non-market sector (the non-industrial public sector) which displaced investment and exports in the market sector. For a clear reference to such models, see Chrystal, Faini and Guiso (1991, pp. 259-63).

[19] It was agreed that compensation would be paid within a relatively short period (10 years). However the new agency lacked the necessary funding, and after only six months of activity, was forced to take on huge debts which seriously compromised its financial management.

introduction of a tax on dividends paid by commercial enterprises, and the establishment of three committees of enquiry (the first on monopoly power, the second on tax reform and the third on economic planning).

In these intricate circumstances there was a widespread conviction that further profound changes would "distort" the system; there were fears in particular of further nationalization. As a result stock market prices slumped, and this marked the start of considerable flows of capital overseas,[20] combined with significant demand-pull inflation. Higher wages, which at least initially were accompanied by monetary illusion, increased purchasing power and boosted demand.

On the monetary front a significant change in the policy stance of the UIC in the spring of 1961 stimulated the creation of monetary base through massive deposits of foreign currency at banks. In addition in January 1962

> the ceiling on compulsory reserves was reduced from 25% to 22.5%: this measure freed 200 billion lire of monetary base. In January 1962 the decision was taken not to renew the nine year treasury bills approaching maturity for a further 100 billion lire. In October of the same year banks were authorised once again borrow overseas. (Spinelli and Fratianni, 1991, p. 510)

The banks responded immediately and overseas bank debt grew dramatically: adjustment of the ceiling was postponed and additional liquidity was created. From this situation it emerged clearly that the monetary authorities were aiming to prevent a current account deficit from reducing the internal money supply.

In January 1963 a total of 200 billion lire was repaid on nine year treasury bills reaching maturity and furthermore banks were authorised to

[20] The reference to Fanno (1935) is immediately evident. This author explains with great clarity the principal motives leading to flows of capital. Both normal and abnormal flows exist: the former arise from the differences in current net interest rates between countries (i.e. without the effects of risk premiums), whilst the latter have various causes and depend on a number of conditions, the most common being: (a) payment of reparations or extinction of foreign debts contracted in times of war; (b) a tax burden greatly in excess of that in other countries; (c) forecasts or fears of an increase in the tax burden; (d) political or social motives; (e) lack of confidence in national banks; (f) fears of devaluation or devaluation of the internal currency. Flows of type (a) are generally initiated by state authorities on the basis of detailed programmes; the others - more irregular and unpredictable - are the result of individual behaviour.

swap long-term bonds with cash and treasury bills held as reserves to guarantee banker's drafts. This freed a total of 100 billion lire of liquidity.

Such a clearly expansionary monetary policy was not justified in the light of the growing external deficit, and the sudden increase in aggregate demand led to a significant price increase: between 1962 and 1963 the balance of payments deteriorated from a surplus of $50.4 million to a deficit of $1,251 million.[21]

From the first quarter of 1963 to the first quarter of 1964 the monetary situation was significantly modified by a conspicuous outflow of capital: banknotes for a total of $1.58 billion were exported, and several similar episodes were subsequently recorded.

A number of instruments were available to policy makers to control aggregate demand. These consisted in reducing public expenditure, introducing appropriate fiscal measures or restricting liquidity.

The first solution was impossible: the Centre-Left government of the day was about to launch a series of important social policies, and could not back out; the economic policy document which was due to be introduced also called for an increase, certainly not a decrease, in public expenditure. Fiscal manoeuvres had generally proved of limited effectiveness in the Italian experience, particularly since the effects were often not immediate and potential delayed effects were counter-productive.[22] So, in an attempt to deflate demand, restrictions on the use of hire purchase were proposed, rather unrealistically considering that hire purchase was beyond the scope of any form of control. The application of customs duties was considered unacceptable given its incompatibility with EEC choices. The only solution was monetary control.

No immediate action was taken, since the monetary authorities continued to pursue their target of full employment and economic

---

[21] This negative result was imputable both to the current account trend and to capital movements. In 1962 legislation was introduced to encourage the purchase of Italian bonds by non-residents, but failed miserably as residents found it profitable to sell the bonds in their possession and repurchase them as non-residents through foreign intermediaries. The result was an outflow of funds rather than an inflow.

[22] In February 1964 fiscal policy included a series of measures which unduly delayed recovery from the recession. On the other hand, as the Monetarist School *à la* Friedman reveals, fiscal measures are associated with long internal delays and shorter external delays, whilst the opposite is true for monetary policy. This accounts for the prevailing opinion that discretionary fiscal measures in Italy accentuated rather than corrected cyclical instability in the economy. For a detailed examination see Cesarano (1980).

development. Only later in 1963 did they opt to safeguard monetary stability and sacrificed these objectives to a limited extent.

In 1964 amid growing concerns over the economic downturn led to the prospect of a possible change of course surfaced.

The various strategies available to policy makers expressed the underlying theoretical foundations from which they derived. Four theories prevailed (Graziani, 1972, pp. 323-4) each advocating a different path.

Supporters of the wage theory argued that the wage explosion was responsible for the downswing, and that increasing wages had jeopardised company budgets, forcing enterprises to increase the retail prices of their products. Advocates of the consumerist theory focused on the under-consumption crisis in the economy. In this case the apparent remedy was an increase in wage levels, in order to "re-launch" aggregate demand by raising consumption. The investment theory stressed the importance of increasing investment, so that aggregate demand could grow. In this context the potential role of state-controlled companies and public corporations was underlined. Finally the monetarist theory was the most neutral of all, advocating credit expansion; however this theory was weak because special credit terms were not potentially strong enough to revive a languishing market.

A range of measures were later introduced, although between 1963 and 1964 the Bank of Italy substantially adopted a severely restrictive monetary policy, generally defined a «credit squeeze». The rate of interest rose from 5.9% in the second quarter of 1963 to 7.6% in the second quarter of 1964; the effect of this rise in the interest rate was a fall in spending on investment.[23] Some of the policies adopted are worthy of note: the tax breaks on a part of social security contributions paid by enterprises (August 1964), the abolition of the tax on the purchase of motor vehicles (October 1964), credit facilities for small and medium sized industrial firms (January 1965) and credits for the purchase of residential dwellings (January 1965).

Meanwhile, certain state agencies, such as the *Ente Nazionale per l'Energia Elettrica* (ENEL, the National Agency for Electrical Energy) and the *Istituto per la Ricostruzione Industriale* (IRI, the Italian Institute for Industrial Reconstruction) pressed for authorisation to issue bonds in order to satisfy their financing requirements. At this point, the authorities

---

[23] If we wish to represent this on the IS/LM curve where IS represents real equilibrium and LM monetary equilibrium, LM shifts to the left and thus in the short term interest rates rise, leading to a contraction of aggregate demand. Over time the fall in expenditure leads to a drop in output and a decrease in the rate of interest.

permitted the banks to purchase medium and long term bonds in order to prevent such bond issues from depressing the stock market and at the same time to squeeze liquidity in the banking sector.

In 1964[24] and 1965 the lending banks took up a remarkable quantity of bonds issued by state agencies, in addition to their purchases of government bonds. This contrasted sharply with the policy of preventing the banks from purchasing medium and long term bonds and prohibiting them from entering capital markets. It was nevertheless true that banks were not authorised to purchase the shares of industrial enterprises directly, but only to acquire bonds issued by credit institutions, which in turn used the proceeds of these issues to finance industrial enterprises. In this way the banks placed liquid funds in medium to long term investments and avoided any direct risks connected with investment in industry.

Thanks to this manoeuvre the desired results were achieved: a fall in interest rates, a reduction in bank liquidity, and increased finance for public corporations and the Treasury. The central bank also had more freedom to engage in open market operations without fear of depressing the stock market excessively. Nevertheless this "simple" monetary manoeuvre, which was not backed up by intervention in the real market, drove the system into a liquidity trap.[25]

From 1964 to 1966 output remained below full capacity, given the scarcity of demand and the presence of idle resources. Direct intervention in the consumer goods market brought signs of recovery. Between 1965[26]

---

[24] From the end of September 1963 a series of measures were adopted to freeze the banks' position on foreign markets at progressively lower levels. Nevertheless since none of the commercial banks had a net credit position on foreign markets the measures were equivalent to sterilising bank reserves. By virtue of the directives imposed by the central authorities, the foreign interest rate trends which discouraged deposits in foreign currency and the rising cost of covering exchange risks, the banks rapidly diminished their foreign debt from $1,200 million in August 1963 to $634 at the end of 1964 (Spinelli and Fratianni, 1991, p. 512).

[25] A liquidity trap (using here Sir Dennis Robertson's expression, which identifies the starting point of infinite elasticity on the demand for money curve) is a situation in which it is believed that the interest rate has reached its lowest level and the price of bonds cannot rise any further. Consequently an increase in the money supply by the central bank cannot make the interest rate fall further, since it does not encourage the purchase of bonds. The liquidity trap is a cause for concern, since in such a state expansionary monetary policy to boost income is ineffective and thus fiscal measures are warranted (Keynes, 1936).

[26] This year marked the start of the growing public debt which for a lengthy period was an extremely delicate issue.

and 1968 substantial monetary stability was enjoyed by the Italian economy (labour productivity increased, and the productive apparatus was rationalised and so on). This stability ended abruptly in 1969. At the start of the year wholesale prices rocketed, fuelled by increases in raw material prices, marking the start of imported inflation. 1969 was a negative year for the Italian economy: the trade unions secured themselves a particularly privileged position in negotiations with the Government.[27]

> Without the "*autunno caldo*" (hot autumn), it has been widely estimated that in 1969 national income would have grown by around 7%: remarkably high and astonishing rate (Mengarelli, 1979, p. 81)

On the contrary, owing to the numerous strikes, national income grew by a mere 5%, the result of irregular bursts of output during the year. Furthermore growth in national income in nominal terms was exposed to inflationary pressure. Inflation was already high at the start of the year and the Bank of Italy was forced to resort to restrictive measures half way through 1969. Although the creation of monetary base by the foreign sector and the banks fell, monetary base created by the Treasury increased. This source of monetary expansion was more dispersive and hence less effective. Monetary policy became even tighter in the first and third quarters of 1969;[28] during these periods the increase in monetary base more

---

[27] Significant action was taken. Parameters for wage negotiations remained in force until the late 1960s; investment incentives for the *Mezzogiorno* weakened the search for cheaper labour abroad. In 1970 the *Statuto dei Lavoratori* (Statute of Workers) was introduced and was of fundamental importance in employment contracts.
At the end of 1992, the proposed re-introduction of wage parameters as a means by which to boost the low productivity rates in depressed areas emerged from the debate over possible "prescriptions" for the country's economic future. Apart from the fact that such measures could do nothing to increase the country's competitiveness, there was also a considerable risk of renewed migration towards the north with subsequent social and economic problems.

[28] In this year there was a renewed outflow of capital overseas, and here a number of interesting considerations emerge. In fact «during the first crisis (1963-64) the remarkable outflow of capital was generally attributed to institutional and fiscal factors (government crises, nationalization of the electricity sector, the introduction of a withholding tax on dividends) and to expectations of devaluation of the lira. Little importance was attributed to the interest rate gap, which at the time was approximately 1% in Italy's favour. In 1969 the capital outflow was mainly the result of speculation (revaluation of the German mark) and the difference between internal interest rates and the eurodollar rate (which

than halved in relation to the previous year and the ratio of liquidity to deposits also fell.

In the fourth quarter of 1969 the renewal of collective contracts for significant categories of workers resulted in sizeable wage settlements which came into effect in January 1970, marking the start of a lengthy period of claims over both remuneration and regulatory aspects. The conflict led to discussion of the possible distortions produced by the sliding scale.[29] The contradictions in the system were revealed fully after

---

was 4 points higher half way through 1969)». (Onida, 1974, p. 85) Later however massive capital outflows continued: this fact was explained by the institutional and fiscal changes and the far from than rosy internal economic outlook.

[29] Sliding scale was introduced in Italy with the inter-confederate trade union agreements of 1945-1946, which aimed to safeguard wages from the loss of purchasing power brought by post-war inflation. This was a rather rudimentary mechanism which operated on a local basis; following the 1951 agreement, it was centralised. The series of regional indicators were replaced by a national allowance point and different values were attributed to an allowance point according to the category, level, age and sex of the worker as well as on the area. At the time it was considered that wage differentials were an important social and economic stimulus. In 1957 a number of changes were introduced, including the adjustment of wages on a quarterly basis rather than a two-monthly basis. Wages became completely index-linked and the rate of price increases was modest. Since there were no damaging price-wage consequences which could potentially have led to a new inflationary spiral, so there seemed to be no relationship between wage indexation and inflation. Later agreements in 1960 and 1963 were essentially concerned with the differentials in the value of the allowance point. Prior to 1975 the degree of coverage was lower, indeed the average rate of coverage of wages was below 50%. With the 1975 agreement the index for the calculation of the sliding scale was updated and the quarter August-October 1974 became the base. The value became the same for all categories of workers, corresponding to the highest white-collar grade. The result was the levelling of wage differentials, one of the motives that induced the various bargaining parties to stipulate the agreement on the cost of labour of 22 January 1983. The value of the allowance point became the same for all workers, but the degree of coverage was reduced. This new line of operation suffered the consequences of the intense debate over neutralisation of the sliding scale (by excluding prices of imported raw materials from the base index). On this issue see Bruni (1981); Monti (1982). From 1986 onwards automatic updating of wages was performed twice a year (in May and November) according to the percentage variation in the trade union allowance point. The increase was applied in full (100%) to a portion of the wage packet for all state and private employees. The remaining portion of the wage packet (excluding production bonuses and seniority increases) was increased by 25% of the index. Thus the cost of living allowance covered only a part of the rise

the oil shocks. In fact in the event of a negative supply shock real wages should fall, but this could not happen in the presence of complete wage indexation.[30]

In these new circumstances, Italy's political forces were confronted with a united working class and with trade unions poised for battle and ready to take whatever action was necessary. The bargaining power of the labour force was considerable, despite large pockets of unemployed or underemployed workers.

The exceptional staying power of the working class and the outstandingly solid organisation of the trade unions effectively counteracted the process of reorganisation, the aim of which was to increase productivity. The trade unions succeeded in reducing the working week and limiting the loss of jobs in the stagnating economy. Firms were faced with rapidly rising unit labour costs and limited growth in demand. They were unable however to recover these cost increases fully by raising prices, without being driven out of international markets. What is more:

> During the 1970's complaints from firms concerning the difficulty of recruiting labour were not infrequent: given the size of the potential pool of labour, the theory of greater market segmentation and a growing diversity between the composition of the demand and supply of labour became highly plausible. (Salvati, 1975, p. 56)

---

in the cost of living. The radical modification of the method of wage indexation led to a lively debate culminating in the suspension of the system on 31 July 1992, in view also of European Union (EU) agreements. The agreement of 3 July 1993 brought radical changes in the determination of the cost of labour. Under the new agreement, wage increases were limited to the programmed level of inflation. The abolition of the sliding scale mechanism benefited Italy in the years between 1992-1994, when, owing to the absence of such a mechanism, the devaluation of the lira did not lead to renewed inflationary pressure. Naturally this was also the result of the anti-inflationary measures which had been introduced.

The Italian experience differed that of other countries. In the United States for example, numerous labour contracts posed limits upon sliding scales linked to the cost of living, at times referred to as COLA (Cost of Living Adjustment) or alternatively wage indexation. Such clauses provided for automatic wage increases in response to increases in the consumer price index. In general wage indexation only partially covered wages. Indeed the United States was less vulnerable to the impact of the oil shocks because of this lower wage indexation.

[30] Goodwin (1982) highlights the role of wage indexation in triggering uncontrollable inflationary dynamics which cause «higher and higher inflation». For an overall critical appraisal of this model see Nardi Spiller (1990b).

It was important to consider the radical changes in the structure of employment: the average age of the workforce fell, workers were not always in line with production techniques, and were of diverse geographical origin as a result of migration. The workforce was now capable of expressing dissent with employers to the extent that trade unions had made their appearance on the shop floor.

2.4 The difficult start of the 1970s

At the start of the 1970s the condition of the Italian economy called for decisive action. There was a specific need to deflate aggregate demand, hence the *gelata di primavera* ("spring freeze", Sylos Labini, 1970) which entailed substantial restriction of monetary circulation and left its mark on the national economy at the start of 1970.[31] This was followed by a distressing phase of stagnation, generated not only by the credit squeeze but also by political and social factors embracing the entire country. In fact,

> We could perhaps say that the credit squeeze sparked the latent crisis inherent in the economy. (Mengarelli, 1979, p. 94)

The view that the aim of restrictive monetary policy was to debilitate the trade union movement seems implausible, particularly since the power of the trade unions had continued to grow in the aftermath of the *autunno caldo*. The sizeable increase in production costs rebounded on prices and profits and sparked a period of recession, as demand faltered; consumption increased only marginally and fixed investments declined. Output stagnated throughout the country and prevented firms, now faced with higher costs, from increasing prices. This effectively mitigated the cost-push inflationary process already underway. If

---

[31] Between 1969 and 1970, the Bank of Italy returned to «leaning against the wind» policies. Such monetary measures of US origin were adopted to counteract the business cycle, and consisted in limiting the creation of money as the economy expanded to limit excessive growth, thereby nullifying inflationary pressure. Conversely, in a recession, measures were taken to boost liquidity and ease recovery. Such policies are effective when the economy is efficient, and when it has a well-developed financial market which transfers monetary impulses to the real sector, and in the absence of balance of payments constraints.

> ....restraint of upward pressure on wholesale prices was evident, it was even more so in the case of capital goods. (*Ibid.*, p. 96)

Regardless of the positive effects of price restraint, investment lacked impetus; indeed by raising interest rates the credit squeeze had its greatest impact on the demand for investment.

Hand in hand with monetary policy came severe fiscal measures,[32] with increases in numerous indirect taxes. The rate of income tax levied on the highest income brackets was raised[33] and the state deficit was also reduced by lowering state demand.

Firms were faced with increasingly scarce financial resources, which created management problems and forced many enterprises to resort to bank loans. In such disconcerting circumstances the banking sector took on a peculiar role, bearing the brunt of increasingly difficult conditions. A new situation evolved in which

> typically private debts of manufacturing enterprises were transformed into debts of state enterprises or enterprises subject to state control. Nevertheless the new corporate powers did not transform, or were not strong enough to transform, the economy based on market freedom and international trade. Nevertheless, with their entry into the spheres of economic and political power, they paralysed certain nerve centres of the capitalist system. (*Ibid.*, p. 98)

Although expansionary monetary policy was adopted once more in the second half of 1970, it was insufficient: at the end of the year the demand for credit was lower than the supply. Fiscal policy made a limited contribution to the expansion of income in this period.

---

[32] During this period the «*Decretissimo*» was introduced. Journalists coined a series of names for the decrees introducing measures adopted by the central authorities to tackle critical issues. A number of interchangeable names were used: the «*Superdecreto*» of 1965, the «*Decretone*» of 1968 and the «*Decretissimo*» of 1970, in addition to the squeezes introduced in later years.

[33] As Salvati (1975, p. 62) claims, in 1970 monetary restrictions were less harsh than in 1963-64, but fiscal policies were far more drastic. The «*Decretissimo*» aimed to ease the pressure of demand on supply by shifting resources from private consumption towards investment. The restrictive effects upon demand were seen immediately whilst the expansionary effects of potential investments were delayed for economic and psychological reasons, the result being a strong deflationary impulse.

In 1971 the full-blown recession brought a decline in gross fixed investment which exacerbated the crisis in the building sector. The situation was worsened by capital outflows[34] in an overall climate of mistrust.

It is particularly interesting to examine the contrast between the trend of investment in machinery and equipment in the periods from 1964-65 and 1971-72. In fact

> they [these investments] were at the centre of the recession, having decreased by 16.9% in 1964 and by 15.6% in 1965. Now there was merely a pause in the rapid rate of growth recorded in 1970: +1.6% and +1.7% in 1971 and 1972 for investment in equipment and machinery only; +3.7% in both years for total fixed productive investment (excluding housing and public works). (Salvati, 1975, pp. 66-7)

Other issues, such as restricted freedom in the organisation of labour[35] had a considerable influence on investment decisions, although problems such as these might appear superfluous in the light of such low demand.

In 1971[36] the slowdown in fixed capital investment and social investment was only partially compensated by public consumption and

---

[34] At the time restrictive monetary policies were coupled with numerous administrative measures inspired by the activist approach, which aimed to halt capital outflows and limit the disastrous effects on the internal economy and the balance of payments. «But even activist approaches – in so far as they have been attempted – have as yet only demonstrated the great ingeniousness with which private capital has found alternative exit routes once the most obvious have been barred; effective administrative measures may require certain political conditions which at the moment do not exist» (Salvati, 1975, p. 73).
Note that although Italy and France belonged to the EEC, both countries maintained severe restrictions on capital movements until 1990.

[35] At the time trade union regulations prevented the introduction of two or three shifts, the use of overtime and transfers of workers between departments or plants.

[36] This year marked the end of the Bretton Woods Agreement. Previously the French President Charles De Gaulle had drawn attention to the unique American privilege of funding political activity and economic expansion through seignorage. Thus in the second half of the 1960s France started exchanging dollars for gold, which led many other countries belonging to the Gold Pool (Belgium, Italy, the Netherlands, Switzerland, West Germany, the United Kingdom and the United States) to sell gold to maintain the parity of $35 per ounce. Official reserves of gold fell, the countries withdrew from the gold market and agreed to buy and sell gold at the official price only among themselves. Gold was traded at a much higher price on the official market, and

investment by state controlled enterprises.[37] Despite the fairly lively export performance, the rate of growth of real income reached its lowest level for 20 years, more than one point below the 1964 level.

Unlike the year 1964, when the marked increase in the cost of labour was gradually absorbed by renewed increase in productivity and a drop in the rate of increase of wages, in 1971 the cost of labour per unit of product (CLUP) recorded a further peak, a consequence of stagnating productivity and of the wage explosion.[38] On the other hand

> Man cannot always resist the temptation of an immediate gain, the consequence of which may be a future loss. (Bresciani Turroni, 1932, p. 289)

The Italian economy embarked upon a period of stagflation[39] which characterised the years from 1971 to 1972.[40]

---

tension was relieved on 15 August 1971 when Richard Nixon suspended convertibility of the dollar into gold.

37 In the context of financing Italian industrial development, particularly in the first half of the 1970s, there was clearly a preference for state finance in many sectors. Cf. Caffè (1984, pp. 387-91).

38 Traditionally CLUP is expressed by the ratio of the cost of labour per hour to productivity per man-hour. If these two variables are both expressed either in monetary or real terms, the ratio gives us information about distribution, whilst if wages and productivity are expressed in monetary and real terms respectively the ratio is used to investigate inflationary aspects.

39 Conditions of stagflation, unempflation and slumpflation seriously undermined the Keynesian model and undermined policy indications deriving from the Phillips curve, which until that time had been thought to explain «reasonably well» the trade-off between inflation and unemployment in no less than 18 countries, including Italy (Lucas, 1973).
The economic impact of the undesirable combination of inflation and unemployment, which particularly in the case of slumpflation is coupled with a drop in output, called for a review of tried and tested models, which proved to be intrinsically fragile. For specific details of these phenomena and related issues see Nardi Spiller (1990a; 1990b, pp. 98-112).
In this context Kaldor (1986) endeavoured to demonstrate how instability, inflation and stagnation at a world level in the 1970s were linked with the inability of the terms of trade of primary and manufactured products to regulate growth rates in the primary (competitive) sector compared to the manufacturing (oligopolistic) sector. This is the origin of the proposal to stabilise the prices of primary products.

40 At the end of 1972 growth in the construction sector was partially the result of administrative measures and partially the result of speculation.

Undoubtedly in the late 1960s the trade union movement became rather aggressive, and this triggered profound changes both in social relationships (Scitovsky, 1978) and in the structure of industry. Indeed between 1956 and 1972,

> the number of disputes increased two and a half fold, while the number of hours lost grew more than six fold, which means that the average length of each dispute more or less quadrupled. (Graziani, 1979, p. 97)

Although tensions accumulated throughout the period, disputes were so intense in the last few months of 1969 that it was labelled the *autunno caldo*. From 1969 to 1973, there was the most rapid and most pronounced redistribution of income between wages and profits observed since the post-war period and it was perhaps only

> from the second half of 1973 onwards [that] the distribution of income in industry favoured profits once more. (Salvati, 1975, 21)

On the other hand

> inflation always has been a terrible tool for redistributing wealth. (Bresciani Turroni, 1931, p. 349)

The trade union struggle had a number of targets - not only wage settlements - so that strikes for various types of reform were staged, including housing, social services, the *Mezzogiorno*, and city transport. Trade union leaders also endeavoured to strengthen their foothold, and this led to the onset of what Graziani (1979, p. 98) has defined a dual wave of conflict, one originating on the shop floor, the other from within the trade union leadership. The impact of the internal shock caused by the aggravation of this social conflict brought about profound changes in the Italian economy, rendering it more vulnerable to external shocks.

2.5 The first oil shock

If we now focus our attention on economic dynamics in the 1970's, critical years for the Italian economy,[41] we observe that the timid recovery of autumn 1971 had lost its impetus by 1972 and was petering out. Internal

[41] For an appraisal of the issues which were central to the Italian economy in the seventies and eighties, see also Nardi Spiller (1990a, pp. 270-7).

demand stagnated as external demand recovered, boosted by the upturn in the international trade cycle. Although the current account of the balance of payments improved, the marked deficit on the capital account was sustained by advance repayments, devaluation of the dollar, loans in dollars, and more profitable foreign interest rates.

Expectations of a devaluation of the lira caused prices to rocket, and this in turn encouraged external operations such as advance payments and delayed collections, starting a process of leads and lags,[42] which had an impact on the balance of payments in both economic and currency terms.[43] At the same time wage rises, the higher level of employment and growing state transfers boosted demand. Indeed the 3% rate of unemployment (typically the rate of frictional unemployment) signalled a return to the level of 1964.

The devaluation-inflation case also deserves attention, within the context of a dirty float. In these circumstances a vicious circle may arise when devaluation of the exchange rate causes internal inflation which destroys any competitive advantage and also hinders adjustment of the balance of payments. Naturally a revaluation-price stability vicious circle may also start in the opposite case, although to a limited extent given the downward rigidity of prices. The devaluation-inflation vicious circle was the subject of debate as early as the 1920's since at the time beggar-my-neighbour policies were adopted to increase exports and reduce imports by certain countries, and such behaviour was generally considered dishonest.

---

[42] In the context of international payments this term indicates advanced or delayed payment in the hope of exploiting expected changes in exchange rates. Thus when a devaluation is expected, residents tend to advance payments to foreigners, who in turn try to delay them.

[43] The economic balance records imports and exports on the basis of data registering the passage of goods through customs and thus not on the basis of payments, as in the case of the currency balance of payments. However following registration on a CIF basis of imports in the currency balance and on a FOB basis in the economic balance, the trade deficit appears to be higher in currency terms.

Until 1992 a distinction was made between the two types of balance of payments. Already by 1990 the balance of payments had changed considerably following the liberalisation of capital movements and from January 1993 customs recorded only trade with non-EC countries, since EC trade was recorded by ISTAT (the Italian Central Statistics Institute) and included operations performed by exporters with annual exports in excess of 150 billion lire. This led to the creation of a single, economic balance of payments using data from various sources including currency data published by the UIC.

Currently two different approaches are used to investigate vicious circles: causality tests and structural macroeconomic models. Causality tests are statistical tests which aim to identify the existence of a link between two variables (i.e. between the exchange rate and the price level). In general terms a variable x causes (statistically speaking) another variable y, if using both past and present values of x, in addition to past values of y, it is possible to obtain a forecast of the current value of y which is better (statistically speaking) than the value we obtain by using only past values of y. If in addition to the fact that x causes y, we obtain that y causes x, the causality link is two-way. Conway, Swamy and Yanagida (1983) challenge the methodological validity of causality tests applied to economic theory. Effectively such tests do not express the economic mechanisms by which we explain the two-way exchange rate-price causality and thus offer no economic policy proposals. Furthermore the tests do not specify whether the circle really is vicious. The second approach tackles the problem by elaborating structural macroeconomic models which consider the relationship between the principal economic variables in order to "explain" the circle, identifying the fundamental cause and the appropriate "cure" to adopt. There are a number of contrasting theoretical positions. Bilson (1979) and Bond (1980) identify the responsibility of monetary policy in sparking off this perverse situation, in an approach which focuses on monetary control. Basevi and De Grauwe (1977) in turn focus on the downward rigidity of prices which thwart possible attempts to introduce restrictive monetary policy. Thus intervention is called for in foreign exchange markets to prevent long-term exchange rate disequilibrium, without causing overshooting effects (Nardi Spiller, 1990b, pp. 141-4). The model offered by Modigliani and Padoa Schioppa T. (1977) is based on a mechanism of cost mark-up pricing as well as a system of price-wage indexation. An exchange rate devaluation determines growth in production costs and thus prices, which is followed by a wage increase and so on. The "cure" consists of intervening in the cost of labour to break the vicious circle.

In the structural model approach, the existence of the vicious circle is proven, although if we seek a plausible explanation a more versatile model which captures the most meaningful aspects of each interpretation would be appropriate. Gandolfo (1986, p. 466) considers the Italian cycle to be convergent in so far as the dirty float constitutes, within limits, a useful policy instrument. Parkin and Bade (1991) note that variations in the nominal exchange rate and the trend of inflation differentials are not closely linked. In fact in recent Italian experience the inflation differential was modest in 1982 but led to a 30% devaluation of the lira, whilst in 1986 the lira appreciated considerably with respect to the dollar despite an inflation differential to Italy's disadvantage.

In the Italian scenario, price rises[44] induced the authorities to introduce a restrictive monetary policy (yet another example of a «leaning against the wind» policy). Despite the credit squeeze there was significant growth in demand in 1973, which spilled over into 1974.

The high priority assigned to development objectives resulted in the creation of a dual exchange market:[45] one for the commercial lira and the other for the financial lira. The Bank of Italy intervened in support of the commercial lira only, and as the financial lira depreciated in the market, capital movements produced effects which were similar to a devaluation, however without the negative impact on prices which an increase in the cost of imports typically causes.

The second dollar devaluation of February 1973, which followed the previous 8% devaluation after the Smithsonian Agreement,[46] and made support of the commercial lira pointless. Italy thus abandoned the «currency snake»[47] and the *de facto* devaluation of the lira gave rise to the

---

[44] Prices rose following the introduction of VAT (Value Added Tax) in October 1972, to replace the sales tax which had been introduced on 9 January 1940 by royal decree.

[45] A dual exchange market was also observed in other states: in Belgium commercial francs and financial francs existed until 1990.

[46] The Smithsonian Agreement of 18 December 1971 led to the realignment of principal currencies, with new fixed exchange rate parities with respect to the dollar, which in August of that year had been declared inconvertible into gold. Fluctuation around par values was increased from 1% to 2.25%. The dollar was devalued, however the international monetary system continued to be based upon the US currency.
After the dollar was declared inconvertible, the United States imposed a 10% surcharge on imports, which it later became possible to abolish as the other currencies realigned. The Smithsonian Agreement thus brought about the realignment of the principal exchange rates.

[47] On the gradual path to European Monetary Union, an attempt was made in 1972 to create an area of monetary stability, known as the «currency snake». The maximum differential between an appreciating currency and a depreciating currency was limited to 2.25%. When it was introduced, the snake was managed as a whole with respect to the dollar, with fluctuations confined to a range of 4.5%. Following the decision taken by a group of EEC countries (in March 1973) to abandon intervention against the dollar, the snake was left to float against the dollar.

so-called «J-effect»[48] in the short-term. The decision to switch from fixed to floating exchange rates was taken at this time, and this period also heralded the start of a process of more or less significant devaluation of the lira against the major foreign currencies.

Devaluation of the lira was not an appropriate instrument to relieve the flagging Italian economy particularly since the Italian productive apparatus was incapable of reacting promptly to the new conditions in the short term.

According to the principle of the efficient classification of markets proposed by Mundell (1961; 1962) in the early 1970s a theoretical approach developed demonstrating that economic strategies could be pursued in a different way. The approach was initially ascribed to Kaldor (1971a; 1971b; 1975) and the debate was continued in a series of articles published in *The Times* newspaper in 1973 and 1974. In Cambridge at the start of the 1970s the New School proposed a new way to allocate instruments to targets. Whilst the Old School assigned the target of internal equilibrium to budget policies and the target of external equilibrium to exchange rate manoeuvres, the New School overturned these ideas (the Cambridge Debate). The new combination was justified by the fact that in processing economies at least, depreciation-devaluation of the exchange rate is an effective instrument with which to stimulate the manufacturing sector, however it may lead to deterioration of the current account of the balance of payments as imports become more expensive and export income contracts. In this view, it would be more appropriate to reduce imports to achieve external equilibrium by means of restrictive budget policy to limit demand.[49]

The experiment was finally abandoned owing to the growing difficulties experienced by member states in managing their inflation and the high costs involved in supporting the adjustment mechanism.

[48] The J-effect is the short term consequence of a devaluation or even a deterioration in the foreign trade balance, caused by delays in the adjustment of quantities traded with respect to values. Such delays depend above all upon the structure of transactions carried out at an international level. In the short term a devaluation of the exchange rate increases the trade deficit, given that quantities imported and exported are inelastic. Subsequently, the increased competitiveness of internal production gradually stimulates exports and may restrain imports. The trade balance reaches equilibrium and there may even be a surplus. In this way the trend of the foreign trade balance comes to resemble the letter J. This explains the idea that a devaluation leads to a long-term improvement in the balance of payments. The J effect is not a recent phenomenon. In fact Fanno (1923) mentions it in the early 1920's. For further analysis cf. Nardi Spiller (1992).

[49] On this subject, see Nardi Spiller (1988).

> To face up to a situation of this kind, Italy needed to offer technologically advanced products, which could compete both with American and with Japanese and German products, instead of hoping to expand sales of 1970s style products, which by now had become «inferior». (Galli and Nannei, 1976, p. 145)

Indeed the fact that Italy pinned its hopes on exports[50] of clothing, household appliances, and cars, failing to keep pace with the times, revealed an excessive trust in the market's acceptance of these goods: the danger was that inappropriate decisions might be taken as a result.

Nevertheless we agree with Salvati (1975, p. 132, footnote 27) who challenges the theory put forward by Galli and Nannei (1974; 1976). The latter authors consider the «Italian financial and bureaucratic-speculating bourgeoisie» to be responsible for the measures which aimed to devaluate the currency. Undoubtedly currency fluctuations and expectations of a devaluation provoked appreciable speculative movements, which however did not represent the cause of the devaluation but rather the "natural" result of behaviour by economic agents to gain speculating from currency movements.

The decision to devaluate the Italian currency aimed to boost demand by triggering a massive rise in Italian exports; this however was not accomplished, and rather inappropriately the fact that such a decision penalised importers was overlooked. The state of the Italian economy at the time was the result of erstwhile measures to curb the upward spiral of industrial costs. In such a delicate situation, it was vital for the central authorities to take prompt and timely action: since curbing growth in industrial unit costs was considered an important target, as soon as signs of a rise in these costs appeared, it became essential to keep this increase on a par with other countries.

The introduction of portfolio restrictions[51] for lending banks was dictated by the need to dampen the long-term interest rate trend. In 1973

---

[50] At the end of October 1973 it emerged that export growth was a mere 17% in the first ten months of the year on a year-on-year basis, compared to 41.4% import growth. According to Galli and Nannei (1976, p. 146) such increases in value, which were not equalled in quantity, were principally the result of higher prices in international markets.

[51] Portfolio restrictions were intended to guarantee the availability of funds for investments in credit instruments expressly designated by the monetary authorities, and to maintain stability in financial markets. Banks were generally obliged to purchase bonds corresponding to a portion of the increase in their deposits. These restrictions were introduced in 1973, relaxed in 1979 and

banks were obliged to increase holdings of government bonds to 6% of their total deposit and current accounts at the end of 1972. This marked the start of a twist policy designed to create a differential between short-term (higher) and medium-term and long-term (lower) interest rates.

It is important to recognise that the recovery in the Italian economy at the beginning of 1973[52] was mainly sustained by inflation and the abundance of money. The economy was unable to spark off a growth spurt from within; the recovery seemed in a certain sense to be "drugged". When the credit squeeze was introduced - yet another example of a «leaning against the wind» policy - the level of output could no longer be sustained, partly the result of the chronic lack of alternative credit and finance facilities.

The oil crisis[53] which began in October 1973 was traumatic for the Italian economy, in terms of the exceptional magnitude of the shock, the drastic measures which were adopted, and the results that were achieved.[54] In Italy the crisis demonstrated how manipulating the exchange rate had a limited effect, owing to the relative price inelasticity of internal and foreign demand at least in the short term (a concrete example of the J-effect). Moreover relative changes in internal and international price levels, which were largely the result of wage indexation,[55] boosted internal

---

abolished at the end of 1986. Portfolio restrictions obliged banks to invest a part of their increase in bank deposits in bonds issued by the ICS (Institute for Special Credit). Conversely lending limits prevented banks from expanding their loan business beyond a certain level. Both of these restrictions forced banks to hold assets in the form of bonds over and above the optimum level.

[52] In 1973 the positive impact on aggregate demand deriving from the increase in the rate of investment was appreciable. Thus despite the credit squeeze, demand grew during the year, and continued to do so until the summer of 1974.

[53] For Hamilton (1983) changes in oil prices played a decisive role in economic fluctuations even before the 1970s. Fortis (1988; 1990) emphasizes the crucial role of some basis products. For an analysis about the Italian situation see Onida (1993).

[54] The interpretation offered by Giavazzi and Spaventa (1989) is particularly interesting. The authors claim that the 1973-1974 energy crisis was followed by a greater recovery in output and an upturn in profitability which preceded other, stronger economies. A more critical view was expressed by Andreatta and D'Adda (1985).

[55] In the event of a monetary disturbance the impact of wage indexation is perfectly neutral on real wages. Conversely when a real disturbance occurs, such as a rise in the price of raw materials, the effects are devastating. During the 1970s many countries, including Italy, encountered adjustment difficulties and experienced inflationary pressure generated by wage indexation. Some scholars argue that the degree of wage indexation in the United States, which was below

output and made it more difficult to redress foreign balances. The income effect compensated the price effect[56] at least partially.

Exchange rate changes can be particularly damaging when they trigger or strengthen a devaluation-inflation-devaluation vicious circle. This in turn magnifies uncertainty in the application of economic policies and the spread of speculative behaviour.

The situation which emerged after the oil shock induced monetary authorities to abandon the long-term interest rate targets which had characterised monetary policy in the 1970's, and to adopt Total Domestic Credit (TDC)[57] as an intermediate target in 1974. TDC remained a priority until 1983.

100%, allowed the American economy to recover more quickly after the oil shocks than other countries. Cf. Bruno and Sachs (1985).

[56] The income effect consists of the increase or decrease in the quantity of a good that is acquired following a change in purchasing power associated with a given level of income, as a result of the price change. The price effect is linked to the demand trend, with increases (decreases) in demand when prices fall (or rise). The substitution effect also occurs when consumers buys more (less) of the good or a price falls (rises) in relation to the price of other goods.

[57] Manipulation of the reserve requirement, discount rate manoeuvres and open market operations were instruments used to influence the supply of credit. These were indirect forms of monetary control. On the other hand direct forms of monetary control included ceilings on the expansion and allocation of credit. Indeed administrative regulation of credit was considered a direct form of control, whilst indirect forms of control were the result of the interaction of market forces (portfolio choices taken by the general public, the behaviour of banks, requests for credit by economic agents). The efficacy of direct controls on the expansion of TDC was given special recognition at the time when economic stabilisation programmes were being agreed with the International Monetary Fund (IMF) for the allocation of stand-by credits. Stand-by credits were granted by the IMF when member states experienced a balance of payments deficit, to allow them to support their exchange rates with foreign currency. TDC was defined as the sum of all bank loans (in lire and foreign currency), special credit institution loans, bond issues by firms and local authorities and the state sector borrowing requirement minus treasury funding of specialised credit institutions. For a detailed analysis of this intermediate economic policy target see Vaciago (1975).

TDC was strictly linked to current account balances, but gradually became less important in the overall determination of the balance of payments as capital mobility increased, particularly after liberalisation. It declined in importance both because it was only controllable to a limited extent by monetary policy and for its limited relevance to the final target (the current account of the balance of payments).

In terms of monetary policy instruments, indirect regulation is achieved if changes in the quantity or composition of credit are the consequence of market forces (open market operations, discount rate, reserve obligations). Direct regulation is achieved via administrative measures (credit ceilings, portfolio restrictions, moral persuasion). Operational targets are variables with which the central bank complies without delay (interest rates on treasury bills). Intermediate targets are variables which are strictly and systematically linked to final targets via the transmission mechanism, so that the central bank treats them as ultimate targets. Such objectives can be formulated in terms of (a) the interest rate; (b) aggregates (the quantity of monetary base; the money stock; the quantity of credit); (c) the composition of bank credit. Final targets are actual objectives to be pursued (full employment of factors of production, growth in real capital, price restraint, equilibrium in the balance of payments). Intermediate targets constitute a link between operational targets and final targets. Instruments are variables that the central bank can control without error and are instruments or parameters over which the monetary authorities exercise legal control (discount rate manoeuvres, reserve requirement manoeuvres and open market operations). Intermediate targets concern monetary variables and influence, with an adequate degree of stability, albeit at times with a certain delay, the decisions of users of economic resources and thus final targets, although it is impossible to establish a connection between specific intermediate targets and single final targets. Since within transmission mechanisms intermediate targets are strictly and systematically linked to final targets, they are considered an end unto themselves by the central bank. Somewhere between instruments and intermediate targets we have operational targets, variables with which the central bank complies immediately. These may included among policy instruments in a general sense, since they are within the control of the central bank. They are not only more closely linked to targets but they may also be directed influenced by instruments (as in the case of the yield on treasury bills). The use of intermediate targets spread in the 1970s as a direct result of both the transition from fixed to floating exchange rates and the generalised existence of high levels of inflation combined with high levels of unemployment. Advance notice of the introduction of such policy measures may be given when programmes are being elaborated for the following year: this may restrict the flexibility of the monetary authorities. On the other hand the announcement may reduce individuals' uncertainty in terms of expectations of the future trend of given economic variables.

Numerous Western economies have in recent experience moved towards more flexible formulation of policy objectives, with tolerances replacing specific values, or periodic revisions of intermediate targets.

> This depended in particular upon the rapid and significant changes in the composition of private portfolios and the growing process of financial innovation. These phenomena, as well as reducing the stability of the relationship between instruments and intermediate targets, have weakened the link between the latter and income. (Predetti, 1990, p. 71)

This preference may have been dictated by the authorities' acceptance of the Keynesian principle of the instability of the demand for money. Volatility in money and financial markets prevented policy makers from focusing action on interest rates to regulate economic activity. Hence the Italian policy makers' decision to control TDC, not only to maintain the interest rate at a low and stable level but also to guarantee accumulation,[58] and thus achieve an effective policy of economic stabilisation.
Nevertheless,

---

[58] In the choice of one or more aggregates as an intermediate target, two factors must be considered: the financial structure (i.e. the type of sources of funds available to firms and the compositions of family financial assets, as well as the stage of development and degree of competition in credit and money markets) and the degree of commercial and financial openness of the economy, hence the possibility of a sufficiently autonomous exchange rate policy. «This means that the choice of a country's intermediate targets depends not only on the different structural and institutional characteristics, but also on the availability of suitable instruments which are capable of effectively influencing relevant variables» (Predetti, 1990, p. 71). There may be several intermediate targets. First and foremost monetary interest rates, i.e. stabilisation over time of, for example, the long-term nominal rate, with the aim of making it easier to finance the deficits of the Public Administration, whilst at the same time maintaining a cost of capital which provides an incentive to fixed private investment. This occurred in Italy above all from the mid 1960s to 1974. Secondly monetary expansion, in both a narrow and a broad sense, in the sense that a constant rate of growth over time of the money supply is achieved, or a range of variation for such growth is fixed. The third intermediate target is TDC, which became important in Italy after 1974, and can be used to control the compatibility of financial and real flows, and can highlight tensions and the probable collapse of equilibrium states. Another intermediate target is Domestic Credit Expansion (DCE), defined as the sum of bank credit and lending (net of deposits) by the Bank of Italy to the Treasury and other sectors which are final users of resources (firms and the public sector). The latter target may be related to the final target of the overall balance of payments. A balance of payments deficit may mean that high growth rates co-exist with moderate expansion of the money supply.
Monetary policy thus may clearly be instrumental in resource allocation, when it specifically concerns the composition of credit, and promote detrimental competition between banks.

> after all we should be aware that if Keynesian policy purports to control a key price variable such as the interest rate while monetarist policy purports to control the quantity of money, the use of a quantitative target, such as controls on the volume of credit rather than a price target, is a monetarist and not a Keynesian policy. (Jossa, 1991, p. 408)

We support this view, while Jossa with Musella (1996) subsequently revised their position and declared that monetarist policies in Italy in fact dated from 1984, when monetary strategy focused on the control of aggregates.[59]

The underlying justification for focusing on TDC was that it was considered more meaningful than the monetary base, which reflected the havoc created by balance of payments deficits - a persistent feature during the oil crises. In terms of the choice of strategy, it was considered that if the instability of the system were of monetary origin,[60] a policy of fixing interest rates would be preferable to a policy of regulating the quantity of money, which in turn would be more appropriate to stabilise income. If stabilising income were the target of economic policy, then the most appropriate measure would consist of fixing the rate of increase of the

[59] The new course of monetary policy was subsequently inaugurated in 1984, when the Bank of Italy announced that the monetary base would become an instrument for regulating economic activity, by strictly controlling the M2 definition of the money supply (Jossa and Musella, 1996, p. 277 and p. 282) as defined below, within the general context of fixing principal monetary aggregates.
The introduction of an authentically monetarist policy was conditional upon the creation of a significant bond market, in order for the public sector deficit to be directly financed by households, leaving the Bank of Italy free to pursue its monetary strategy.

[60] Here the explicative approach derived from the Poole (1970) model is relevant. This author's choice of an appropriate instrument in a closed economy with the assumption of constant prices is based on the minimisation of fluctuations in income around the level taken as average during cyclical fluctuations, which represents a target. In this way monetary policy should aim to maintain the value assigned to the «quantity of money» instrument (leaving interest rates free to vary endogenously) if the transitory shock derives from fluctuations in expenditure in real markets. Conversely if the transitory shock derives from financial markets then policy should aim to maintain the value assigned to the «rate of interest» instrument. For analysis of this model see Arcelli (2000, pp. 273-82).

money supply in conditions of real instability in the economy and in stabilising the interest rate in conditions of monetary instability.[61] Indeed

> even an aggregate as broad as TDC does not allow interest rates to be stabilised in the face of major exogenous shocks. (Spinelli and Tullio, 1982, p. 19)

Interestingly, during the policy of stabilisation, the banks actually opted to purchase bonds: such an attractive opportunity to invest in bonds induced the banks to raise their interest rates on deposits. This in turn persuaded the general public to opt for bank deposits rather than purchasing bonds.

The currency devaluation caused serious problems, and these were reflected in the stance adopted by the central authorities. Massive intervention by the central bank

> reduced the rate of devaluation of the lira compared to levels probably found in unregulated exchange markets. Defending a given external value of the lira was considered an important instrument within this complex system of intervention. On the other hand however the authorities continued to reject the re-entry of the lira into the currency snake, despite requests from all sides, particularly since the beginning of the year. Re-entry would have led to the revaluation of the lira, pulled by the other stronger currencies. (Garavello, 1977, pp. 178-9)

The refusal to return to the «currency snake» was motivated by the need to gain stronger support, allowing the lira to be pegged to the main European currencies; there was also clearly an urgent need for united action against the dollar. A mechanism was also required to allow weaker currencies to temporarily leave the currency snake without such events becoming traumatic.

In 1974 the cyclical trend was particularly contradictory: at the start of the year strong output growth pushed up prices and generated a significant balance of payments deficit. At the close of the year output fell considerably, the external balance[62] improved and a degree of price

---

[61] There is no evidence to support the Keynesian hypothesis of the inherent instability of financial markets.

[62] The introduction of an interest free deposit on imports, equal to 50% of their total value for a period of six months, contributed to the improvement of external balances. Investment goods and raw materials were exempted from the deposit requirement, which effectively reduced imports and increased their cost

restraint was achieved, partly the result of price controls. These difficulties induced policy makers to negotiate stand-by credits with the IMF. As the discount rate increased, it limited expansion of the monetary base and helped to bring short-term rates back in line with prevailing rates in international markets. There was no longer any need to maintain two exchange rates and the new exchange rate settled close to the value of the commercial lira.

With the cyclical downswing at the end of the year, a more expansionary credit policy was adopted (with a cut in the discount rate, as well as the adjustment of credit ceilings[63] and the reserve requirement). Profound changes also came about in the structure of society. Italy had traditionally been a net exporter of manpower, however in 1974 this situation reversed as the nation became a net importer. This curious phenomenon was the result of immigration bans imposed by a number of countries in 1973, including Germany, as well as the return home of Italian emigrants and the influx of foreign workers from African nations in particular.[64]

---

by means of a drain on liquidity. The introduction of the deposit on imports was effectively a form of selective credit control to reduce balance of payments tension. It became compulsory to deposit cash equal to a given percentage of the value of imports. In addition to this liquidity squeeze far-reaching fiscal and tariff measures were introduced in July 1974. Such measures proved to be excessively restrictive.

[63] The regulation of credit, especially between 1973 and 1983, was achieved principally by resorting to administrative measures, such as bank credit ceilings and portfolio restrictions, which had an impact on the cost, quantity and composition of credit. The ceilings, which consisted of limits on the expansion of bank loans, had a rationing effect and influenced the real decisions of firms, by affecting their financial structure. The latter aspect is emphasised in the Credit View, but rejected in the Money View. For a comparison, see Pittalunga (1999, pp. 294-7). The ceiling was suspended in 1983, re-introduced in the first semester of 1986, once again in September 1987 and March 1988, and was then permanently abolished.

[64] It is difficult to maintain that immigration can produce the effects predicted by the Lewis-Kindleberger model, in which the increase in the supply of labour lowers wages and limits trade union power. See Lewis (1954); Kindleberger (1967), and for an explanation of the model, Valli (1990, pp. 208-15). In reality this effect, which is probably unlikely in the short-term, is also unlikely in the long-term since competition from immigrants does not constitute a real threat to better qualified domestic workers. Possible competition may affect the black economy. The detailed approach of the Structuralist School offers a satisfactory explanation (Nardi Spiller, 1996).

In 1975 problems inherited from previous years came to the fore,[65] in the form of unempflation, with rocketing prices were coupled with rising unemployment. In 1975, and to a greater extent than in the recessions of the 1960s and 1971-72, personal disposable income increased in relation to national income, somewhat surprisingly. The explanation for this can be found in the rapid increase in transfers during the period, whilst growth in income tax fell. Between 1960-1990, the ratio of disposable income to national income was on average 80.7% (Dornbusch and Fischer, 1992, p. 483).

The agreement on the sliding scale of January 1975 led to the unification of the allowance point and effectively guaranteed considerably higher coverage of wages compared to price increases in the previous period.[66] As Spinelli (1980) notes, the debate on the size of the inflation rate coefficient in the wage equation was rendered futile by this agreement.

The balance of payments required urgent adjustment, and at the same time there was a pressing need to boost output and slow price growth. A number of monetary and financial manoeuvres were introduced (including an overhaul of the reserve requirement system, a commitment to create a more efficient money market a suspension of the interest free deposit on imports and a reduction in portfolio restrictions).

---

[65] In that year the Bank of Italy was obliged to purchase any residual treasury bills, at its own terms, in the monthly auctions. The result was that the monetary base became more dependent upon the often unpredictable requirements of the Treasury (Sarcinelli, 1981, p. 443). It is also important to remember that until 1975 the monetary base included treasury bills deposited in the reserve requirement. Furthermore in 1975 Guido Carli ended his term as Governor of the Bank of Italy (1960-1975). This was significant, because a different approach to the application of monetary policy subsequently became apparent. For example the refinancing of banks could be regulated either directly or indirectly. In the first case, the central bank agrees or refuses discounts and loans at its discretion. In the latter case the bank operates through changes in the discount rate. Under Carli, regulation was mainly direct, whilst under Carlo Azeglio Ciampi (Governor from 1979 to 23 April 1993, when he became Prime Minister) regulation was principally indirect.

[66] The model of an open economy formulated by Modigliani and Padoa Schioppa T. (1977) mentioned above, prospected an «infernal cycle» for the Italian economy. The inflationary process had a negative impact on the balance of payments and led to a fall in income and employment. Devaluation of the lira fuelled the external account deficit and was encouraged by those who favoured devaluation. The restrictive measures warranted by the inflation rate led to unemployment and stagnation. The result was a downturn which stimulated a new expansionary policy, which in turn led to inflation and so forth.

Demand contracted following a fall in private consumption and a reduction in investment. A number of measures to boost output were introduced, including specific measures for the *Mezzogiorno*. However such intervention did not succeed in counteracting the decline in industrial activity. The industrial production index was 12% lower at the end of the year than the previous year.[67]

In an effort to kindle demand, the «Visentini fiscal mini-reform» was introduced to curb, if not to erase, fiscal drag[68] on progressive personal income tax rates caused by inflation. The effects were inadequate and in 1975, for the first time since the Second World War, GDP fell sharply.

In 1976[69] the economic recovery was boosted by the restocking of inventories, with a consequent rise in the level of imports. This generated tension in external balances and revealed the fragility of the economy, which needed to reconcile external constraints with healthy internal growth rates. The currency depreciation (following closure of the foreign

---

[67] The unsatisfactory real growth in the Italian economy can be considered an indicator of the negative impact of the first oil shock which resulted in a deterioration of the terms of trade. Cf. Fazio (1979, p. 316).

[68] As defined by Heller (1967, p. 65) fiscal drag is the appearance of a fiscal dividend which is not allocated either to tax reductions or increased expenditure. More generally, fiscal drag indicates the phenomenon whereby given the progressive nature of direct taxation, as income increases the portion withheld by the government also increases. This effect has negative repercussions upon demand and consequently also upon supply. Curiously the phenomenon of progressive taxation is ever more closely linked to inflationary dynamics. The latter causes nominal income to rise and so moves tax payer's personal income into higher tax brackets. The real increase in tax revenue deriving solely from inflation is due to bracket creep. Thus inflation interacts with a system of progressive taxation, shifting tax payers' monetary income towards higher brackets.

[69] The agreement reached in Kingston (Jamaica) in 1976 ratified the system of flexible exchange rates and allowed the United States to achieve its objective of eliminating gold from the international monetary system. The situation which followed effectively marked the end of the Bretton Woods System, and sharp short-term and long-term exchange rate fluctuations were experienced. In the mid-seventies, for example, the dollar was undervalued, and it was generally believed that this was the result of the excessively expansionary American policy. The subsequent turnaround led to the overvaluation of the dollar. Between 1981 and 1985, the dollar became overvalued by 69% with respect to the mark and 120% with respect to the lira. More recently, it has been thought that this instability was the result of capital flows. Thus the overvaluation of the dollar (1979-1983) determined high interest rates and attracted considerable capital inflows.

exchange market from 20 January to 27 February) benefited exports whilst imports were once again penalised by the introduction of an interest free deposit paid in advance and equivalent to 50% of the value of imports.

> In particular, the currency crisis of January 1976 may be considered the penalty to be paid for having attempted to set the economy back on an expansionary path too rigidly after several quarters of acute recession, at a time when the economy was slow in reacting to the wage and oil shocks, which in fact called for thorough reorganisation of the output structure. (Signorini and Visco, 1997, p. 63)

A compulsory foreign currency loan equal to 30% of the value of imports with deferred collection was also introduced, and was increased to 50% in October. It remained in force, albeit with some minor changes, until June 1978. Imports were also restrained by increasing the reserve requirement coefficient and the official discount rate, both of which restricted liquidity. However the pressure on the balance of payments was such that in autumn of that year severe fiscal and tariff measures were introduced, together with monetary and foreign exchange intervention. The discount rate was raised and a special duty of 10% was imposed on sales in foreign currency which were in any case gradually abolished as a result of strong opposition both from the EC and the IMF.

> The restrictive nature of monetary policy was demonstrated not only by the increase in nominal interest rates but also by the higher ratio – highlighted in data from the Central Risks Department of the Bank of Italy – of credit used to credit allocated among enterprise: this index is particularly representative of the extent of credit rationing. (Gambale, 1986, pp. 271-2)

Income, which in real terms was marginally above the 1974 level, showed signs of a recovery rather than of an actual increase.

The early months of 1977 confirmed the timid recovery witnessed at the end of the previous year. The introduction of a number of fiscal measures[70]

[70] The stop-go policy of British origin applied to the trade cycle and introduced into Italy above all in the 1970s involved the application of fiscal and monetary incentives when high levels of unemployment, unemployment existed, and sudden disincentives as inflationary pressure appeared. Such policy was strictly related to the balance of payments trend. Indeed in an expansionary phase it is likely that the balance of payments will show a deficit, so that the expansion must be halted (stop), to reduce imports. The elimination of the deficit boosts

was coupled with efforts to limit CLUP. These fiscal measures included self-assessment for income tax, introduced in 1976, followed by compulsory advance payments for IRPEF (Personal Income Tax), IRPEG (Corporation Tax), ILOR (Local Income Tax) and a withholding tax on interest income. At the same time changes were made to the cost of living index, and tax breaks were granted on a portion of social security contributions paid by industrial enterprises. Italy also obtained stand-by credits from the IMF. Imports were restricted by the limited availability of credit, and the elasticity of imports with respect to industrial production became negative (-1.8), having been stable at around 1.3 for the previous 15 years (Gambale, 1986, p. 272). The discount rate was lowered gradually and tax breaks on social security contributions were extended from industry[71] to include the commercial sector, albeit partially.

The weak revival of demand, stabilisation of the exchange rate and the standstill in raw material imports assured an improvement in external balances and combined to slow the rate of price increase. Nevertheless there was a substantial increase in the enlarged public sector deficit[72] with respect to the target indicated in the letter of intent (21,000 billion lire against 16,450). TDC also increased beyond previously agreed levels.

In 1978 the balance of payments recorded a surplus, mainly the result of current account transactions. External and internal demand jointly contributed to the growth of national income, which previously had suffered the strongly negative impact of the oil shock upon the terms of trade.

---

recovery of investment (go), until renewed balance of payments problems arise. Such policy measures are well-suited to analysis of balance of payments equilibrium following the absorption approach put forward by Alexander (1952).

[71] Law 675 approved in August 1977 established the *Fondo per la Ristrutturazione e Riconversione Industriale* (Industrial Restructuring and Reorganisation Fund) and brought benefits to the manufacturing structure.

[72] The concept of the enlarged public sector was introduced in the mid 1970s and was an important aggregate in quantitative and qualitative terms for measuring state intervention in the economy. It comprises government agencies (central and local government and social security institutions), autonomous agencies producing services for sale (telephones, state monopolies and the postal service), the railways and the national electricity corporation. For analysis of the situation in Italy see Cavazzuti (1979).
The definition used for the public sector is different to that used in consolidated national accounts in terms of the minor government agencies (Banca d'Italia, 1992, *Appendice*, p. 73*).

This positive change of course had a beneficial effect upon prices, which grew less than the previous year, partly the result of the lower rate of increase in CLUP, explained by the lower allowance point on the sliding scale.

In terms of wages, great importance was attributed to the publication of an interview with Luciano Lama, then leader of CGIL (General Confederation of Italian Trade Unions), in the *La Repubblica* daily newspaper. In the interview Lama admitted that the hard line adopted by the unions in previous years had been misguided, not only in relation to the actual state of the country but also in terms of its theoretical foundation. He added that wage claims, an independent variable,[73] which had up to that time been ferociously defended, were misconceived given that «in an open economy all variables are interdependent». This statement led to a radical change in labour relations. In fact at the CGIL annual general meeting of middle management held in the EUR suburb of Rome in February 1978, the so-called «EUR line» of policy prevailed. The «EUR line» censured behaviour which aimed to increase productivity and boost employment by means of increased labour mobility, in exchange for more incisive economic planning and greater «industrial democracy». This line of policy implicitly sanctioned the entry of the Italian left-wing parties into the Government. Indeed

> The analytical framework underlying the EUR line outlined in the policy document is peculiarly similar to the policy advocated by the Bank of Italy in the 1960's. The fundamental objective is full employment. (Valli, 1999, p. 149)

The strengthening of external balances offered the authorities a certain degree of interest rate independence in relation to trends in international markets. Interest rates in capital markets once again exceeded short-term rates, reflecting the need to extend maturity on public debt into the longer term.

---

[73] In this context we can link up to Sraffa's analysis. Sraffa (1960) states that it is possible to determine, on the basis of technological considerations (labour and technical coefficients) in the production of goods, relative prices of all goods and a distributive variable (wage or profit rate), starting from the other exogenously determined distributive variable. Thus the implication for economic policy is that since the distribution of income is an exogenous variable that cannot be determined by the model, we must consider wages an independent variable.

Growth in public expenditure was rather rapid, rising from 32% to 50% of GDP between 1970 and 1979. This spiral prevented state finance[74] from influencing cyclical phenomena and hence the trade cycle. The state budget was effectively transformed from an instrument for regulating demand into a target in itself.

The demand for credit eased. In the light of the credit ceilings and the growing government borrowing requirement, banks increased their absorption of the total supply of government bonds.[75]

The rate of growth of the public deficit decelerated with the first introduction of the financial act (Law 468/1978) coupled with substantial changes in the system of government accounting which aimed to limit the pressure exerted on prices, the balance of payments and resource allocation by public finance.

By the end of 1978 the Italian economy had accomplished its programme to stabilise the foreign trade balance and thus was in a position to tackle the issue of reabsorbing unemployment. In such conditions a policy of moderate wage growth was considered essential for stability of real labour costs and greater labour mobility. It became quite clear that the current deficit in state balances would have to be restrained if greater resources were to be dedicated to investment.

2.6 The second oil shock

At the end of 1978[76] and the start of 1979 demand became buoyant once more. 1979 was an important year for the EC and on 13 March the European Monetary System (EMS), which Italy had joined in 1978, came

[74] Valiani (1979) analyses the variations in public finance recorded between 1957-1977 in Italy, and underlines how the increase in government expenditure was superior to the increase in GDP. In his study he identifies tax-payers' resistance to an increase in fiscal pressure and the existence of decreasing social returns associated with large social and public expenditure programmes, and finally attributes a significant role to the possible negative effects upon economic activity of the growth in government expenditure and taxation in relation to GDP.

[75] In the second half of the year portfolio restrictions were reduced from 30% to 6.5% of the increase in deposits.

[76] In August 1978 the Finance Minister Pandolfi presented a draft medium-term programme, which was later amplified and in January 1979 became the 1979-1981 Three Year Plan (or Pandolfi Plan). Although the plan mentioned a number of traditional targets which were typical of Italian planning (territorial imbalances, employment and so on) it pivoted on the issue of inflation and was effectively a plan for curbing inflation. Cf. Documento Pandolfi (1978).

into operation, thus contributing to the "building" of European Monetary Union (EMU).[77]

Nevertheless rising international raw material prices - particularly the price of oil - in the aftermath of the political events in Iran and negotiations over the new labour contract led to a drop in output in the

---

[77] With Italy's entry into the EMS, intermediate policy targets were pursued alongside the nominal exchange rate target. The EMS aimed to consolidate monetary stability between member states. The minimum and maximum rates at which intervention became compulsory were fixed around an agreed par value, with a 2.25% fluctuation margin. Until January 1990 the lira was allowed a margin of 6%. In 1992, the pound, the peseta and the escudo were also exceptionally allowed a wider margin of 6%.
For a detailed investigation of the changes over time in the process of wage determination following Italian membership of the EMS see Baici and Dell'Aringa (1994). The model presented in this essay attributes a fundamental role to the rate of unemployment as an indicator of excess demand in the labour market.
On 1 August 1993 an agreement was concluded in Brussels establishing 15% fluctuation margins. This decision effectively marked the end of the system of fixed exchange rates, an integral part of the Maastricht Agreement. With the signing of the European Union Treaty, which had been approved on the night between 11 and 12 December 1991, signed on 7 February and was ratified in 1993, a number of fundamental choices were made. The agreement concerned the extension of the EC's field of action and redefined roles and relationships between institutions. A central role was attributed to currency management. The agreement set a number of fixed targets for the accomplishment of the single European currency (3% government deficit/GDP ratio, ceilings on interest and inflation rates and a 60% public debt/GDP ratio). At the same time the principle of subsidiarity was upheld, so that decisions were to be taken by governments which were as close as possible to citizens, and only when objectives could not be satisfactorily fulfilled by member states would the EC (European Comunity) intervene. The agreement was not just monetary, since in many areas it foresaw a gradual shift of power from member states towards the EC. Nevertheless «It must be said that in all this agreement is too biased towards monetary and financial objectives, and rather narrow and lacking innovation in terms of the real economy (such as industrial and technological policy, social policy and vocational training), and the need to achieve rapid integration in Central and Eastern Europe» (Valli, 1999, p. 51). Under the Treaty national regulatory power was limited without an adequate compensatory structure of regulatory tools at a community level. On the other hand by upholding the independence of central banks, the agreement established that institutions in countries joining EMU could not grant national governments any form of credit and neither could they purchase government securities in the primary market. The Treaty was ratified by fifteen member states of the Union, whilst only eleven nations adhered to EMU.

second quarter of 1979. In that year the Iranian crisis sparked the second oil shock with negative repercussions on the Italian economy, although this time a certain positive responsiveness emerged, unlike the previous shock.

In the third quarter of 1979 there was significant recovery, stimulated by the need to restock inventories and by the higher level of liquidity.

The increase in the price of oil[78] imposed by OPEC in mid 1980[79] led to massive speculative dollar movements followed by devaluation of the dollar. In September the central parities of EMS currencies were realigned.

Inflationary expectations pushed up interest rates in money markets, ceilings on bank credit were extended and the discount rate was raised. This indicated

> an explicit return to managed interest rates in order to defend the external value of our currency. (Confederazione Generale dell'Industria Italiana, 1980, p. 54)

Industrial production grew despite the restrictive monetary policy, the trade deficit also grew. The 20% annual rate of price growth evinced a disturbing inflationary trend.

2.7 The problems of the 1970s

The main explanation put forward for the inflationary trend which characterised the Italian economy in the early 1970s in particular was the heated conflict in the labour market. This in turn was the result of greater trade union bargaining power, taken as an exogenous variable, which made the economy more vulnerable to external shocks. In this approach the money supply had no direct and independent effect upon inflation, although the banking system was to be ready to

> finance, directly or indirectly, the private or public sector, by increasing the money supply. (Sylos Labini, 1972, pp. 79-80)

---

[78] At times a parallel is drawn between indirect taxation and an increase in the price of oil, and we even speak of an oil tax. Apart from the clear distinction between the latter and a tax burden, the comparison is totally misconceived. Taxation "generates" funds which should later return to the system. A increase in the price of oil does not give rise to any internal redistribution of income, but rather favours only the exporting countries of this strategic raw material.

[79] The price of crude oil was more than ten times higher than pre-1973 levels at $32 a barrel.

This interpretative model was later criticised,[80] since it was considered impossible for market forces, in this case the trade unions, to continuously fuel such substantial wage growth. The monetarist stance held the inflationary expectations which predominated the automatic mechanism of the sliding scale[81] to be responsible.

It is important not to underestimate the relevance of public expenditure in crowding out private expenditure.[82] In this context

80 See among others Spinelli (1976; 1980); Fratianni (1980).

81 Spinelli and Zis (1979) fiercely criticised the model proposed by Modigliani and Tarantelli (1973), and reached the conclusion that in Italy no long-term trade-off between wage-push inflation and unemployment existed.

82 The somewhat satirical empirical postulate regarding the public apparatus known as «Parkinson's Law» identifies a curious situation, in which the principal purpose of bureaucracy is to enlarge itself regardless of its official function: the workload increases as a function of the increase in the size of the organisation. See Parkinson (1980).

In the 1970s when Italy experienced an absolute and relative increase in public expenditure and revenue, a number of possible explanations were offered. Reference was made to «Wagner's Law» (1912), whereby the ratio of public expenditure to national income tends to expand as income rises (Giannone, 1983). This is justified by the fact that the services offered by government authorities are superior goods, i.e. goods with elasticity of demand with respect to income greater than 1. Hence this law is included among the structural, social or functionalist models, given that the expansion of public expenditure is a natural phenomenon caused by economic growth and the structural evolution of society. In the Baumol's model (1967), low productivity increases in the public sector mean that the sector tends to increase relatively in size. This model belongs to the so-called structural models, not on account of its reference to the structure of society but rather to public sector output.

O'Connor (1973) offers an approach in which the fiscal crisis derives from the fact that enlargement of the oligopolistic sector of the economy requires, either directly or indirectly, an increase in public expenditure which is not wholly compensated by an increase in tax revenue. The higher level of expenditure is in theory related on the one hand to an increase in public support to the oligopolistic sector and on the other to the increase in social expenditure needed to gain or maintain popular support. In this scenario, it would be natural to refer to political-business cycle theories which signal the preferences of politicians, given that each political party assigns different priorities to economic targets for reasons of political ideology, particularly considering the diverse goals of the social groups that they represent (Alesina, 1987). Thus even when information is the same, strategies are different. The political-electoral cycle approach (Nordhaus, 1975) stresses the importance of efforts by politicians to ensure re-election, with a marked increase in activity as the elections approach in order to

crowding-out[83] became the central theme in the debate between the Keynesian and Monetarist Schools. Crowding out emerged in the 1970's when administrative tools were first introduced to regulate financial flows and alter distribution between the public and private sectors (Arcelli and Valiani, 1979).

In the 1970's seigniorage[84] reached exceptional levels for a peacetime economy and in fact

---

preserve their vested power. Kalecki (1975) focuses on the possibility of increasing growth in income through public expenditure, which however is opposed by industrial leaders for ideological and socio-political motives. Maintaining full employment would promote greater self-assurance among blue collar workers, weaken the disciplinary function exerted by fear of losing one's job and encourage industrial action. This would lead to risky political and social changes. Class conflict encouraged by full employment would not lead to a fall in profit, or at least not necessarily, given the ability of firms to pass on the increased cost of labour in the form of higher prices. However factory discipline and political stability are appreciated more than profit. Class instinct considers full employment to be "unhealthy" and unemployment to be an integral part of the capitalist system. On the other hand the role of unemployment as a disciplinary tool is even emphasised in the shirking model (Shapiro and Stiglitz, 1984). Once more in the context of increasing public expenditure, the displacement effect tends to explain the expansion of public expenditure in leaps. With a substantially balanced government budget, increases in public expenditure are limited by the maximum tolerable level of tax pressure. However the latter may shift upwards discontinuously and then remain fixed at a new level by a process of custom. For a detailed analysis of the Italian budget policy in the second half of the 1970s see OECD (1980).

[83] Crowding-out is the opposite of crowding-in. Just as yields on treasury bills are higher than the interest rates at which banks and specialised credit institutions attract funds, it is also true that the cost of loans granted by the latter are lower. This gives rise to the private crowding-in effect, as well as offering opportunities for arbitrage between investments in government securities and bank debt. See Friedman B. (1978); Arcelli and Valiani (1979) and Valiani (1979).

Super crowding-out may occur when the value of the multiplier is negative. Additionally, despite a multiplier greater than 1, partial crowding-out may occur in relation to certain variables: thus investments may fall although consumption rises.

[84] This phenomenon was significant in Italy until 1976, then fell to a marginally negative percentage between 1993 and 1995.

The government "extracts" seigniorage by transforming part of the public debt into money, whilst it levies an inflation tax when the primary real borrowing requirement exceeds the overall increase in deflated debt. The primary borrowing requirement is calculated by subtracting interest expenses from the

> on average it accounted for 6.1% of income, compared to 1.6% in the 1950s and 1960s and 3.6% for the whole of the period from 1862-1980. The highest level of seigniorage was recorded in 1976 when it touched 15%. (Spinelli and Fratianni, 1991, p. 550)

Within the complexities of the Italian situation, we should always bear in mind that the energy issue imposed strict limits upon what was a predominantly processing economy.

On the other hand focusing attention on one aspect in a particularly significant period may undermine other important but less pressing aspects which are part of the system or have determined a certain course of events. The causes of Italian inflation were not immediately apparent because many potentially relevant justifications existed both on the cost and the demand side, with significant interrelationships. This type of explanation, of Keynesian origin, was combined with the growing role of expectations, affecting both the price level and the exchange rate, as well as potential incoherence in monetary and fiscal policy.[85]

The expansionary phases of 1976 and 1979-80 were years in which significant foreign trade deficits necessitated restrictive measures, which were later the cause of recessions (1977 and 1981). In this case, unlike the 1960s (1963 deficit and 1964 recession) a number of peculiarities were observed: high inflation[86] coupled with a disappointing GDP trend, so

---

total borrowing requirement. Masera (1986), Spinelli and Fratianni (1991) obtain similar results for seigniorage over time. The rate of inflation rose from the negative values averaged in the 1960s to the all time high of 6.6% of GDP in 1976.

[85] Fratianni (1980) hypothesises a cost-push model with a Phillips curve on one side and a mark-up equation on the other and concludes that for the estimate period (1952-1977) the monetarist framework offers a better interpretation of inflation in Italy than the cost-push approach. Nevertheless Guiso (1984) notes how the cost-push model estimated by Fratianni fails to satisfy certain criteria of statistical acceptability. He immediately goes on to say: «The price equation contains a degree of residual self-correlation to which Fratianni seems to pay no heed» (*Ibid.*, p. 33). Also see Guiso (1984) for an analysis of the differences between versions offered by Spinelli (1976; 1980; with Zis, 1979) and Fratianni (1978; 1980), although both approaches hinge on the hypothesis that the inflationary impulse stems from the rate of growth of the money supply.

[86] In the 1960s in addition to the problems encountered by the principal economies concerning the appropriate combination of fiscal and monetary policies, these countries were also faced with speculative bubbles and peso problems.

much so that a GDP gap[87] emerged. A unique feature of the Italian economy is the household propensity to save, although this has been falling in recent years. In the 1960s Italian households saved on average marginally less than 12% of GDP;[88] in the 1970s the household propensity

History provides many examples of speculative bubbles: the tulip craze of the 17th century, the rocketing stock market prices before the crashes of 1929, 1987 and 1989 and the prices of building land in Japan in the late 1980s to name but a few. Bubbles are persistent movements in the price of an asset away from its core value or from what is perceived to be its core value. A bubble cannot form when the real price of a security becomes so high or so low that it affects the real sector: the activity of forward-looking agents will prevent this. See Burda and Wyplosz (1993, pp. 639-43). Flood and Garber (1980) attempted to verify whether bubbles are reflected in price data. The role of speculative bubbles as a component of the workings of macroeconomic models is investigated by Blanchard and Watson (1982). For a historical appraisal of bubbles see Chancellor (1999).

In the 1980s the peso problem (typical of Argentina) arose when expectations of the most important trends affected the current exchange rate. See Kaminsky (1993).

[87] In the 1970s the growing role of the black economy became apparent and indeed it was considered of fundamental importance in Italian growth. «Four paths have led to the industrialisation of Italy: traditional capitalism, state shareholdings, assisted capitalism, and hidden industry» (Saba, 1980, p. 15). With no data available, it is impossible to estimate the contribution in quantity terms to production. Deaglio (1987) affirms that from 1970-1985 there was significant hidden activity in the textile, clothing, leather and shoe sectors, as well as in the food, beverage and processed tobacco sectors. There was also evidence of hidden activity in the timber industry. The black economy is not confined to Italy. Siesto (1987) reveals that Italy is in fact in fourth place behind Sweden, Belgium and Denmark. A black economy is also to be found in the Netherlands, France, Norway, Austria, Canada and the United States (*Ibid.*, p. 23).

[88] In France and Germany the propensity to save was 7.8%, in the United Kingdom only 3.8%, and in the United States it fluctuated between 4%-5%. During this period only Japan had a higher propensity to save than Italy.

At this point it is worth remembering the problems which the management of savings can bring. Banks' portfolio management is sluggish, and even more so are the pension funds of social security institutions. This uniquely Italian situation can be explained by the rapid increase in bank deposits in the 1970s, the high demand for government bonds in the 1980s and early 1990s, currency trends (in particular between July 1973 and May 1987), the volatility of the Milan stock exchange, the delay in enacting the law on unit trusts and the lack of legislation on private pension funds. In the currently evolving situation

to save[89] rose between 1970 and 1978 and fell sharply between 1978 and 1980. After 1980 it rose once more, and then fell again in the 1990s.

further significant changes may come about and the role of money managers may become significantly more important.

[89] Financial brokerage expanded considerably until 1973, partly the result of the high propensity to save, and partly the result of the financial policy to promote development pursued in particular by Governor Carli: this favoured the accumulation of capital by increasing the money supply, expanding credit and granting special credit facilities.

3. Problems Old and New

A placid philosophy leads me by the hand, and I consider the elements of national prosperity as we might consider the laws of motion. (Verri, 1910-42, p. 25)

3.1 The tensions of the 1980s

In the 1980s the Italian economy bore a heavy burden: a tangle of monetary, financial and real problems inherited from the past, for which no easy solution existed.[1] On one side were the principal external

[1] In terms of the correct measurement of inflation, at the start of the 1980s the base rate of inflation hypothesis (Pendersen and Karnosky, 1977; Parkin, 1978) met with increasing consensus. The base rate reflected traditional price changes which stemmed from the fundamental causes of the inflationary process. Unlike estimates based on price indexes, identification of the base rate of inflation is strictly related to the interpretative approach of the causes of inflation, and examines monetary causes. In this approach money plays a dual role in price growth: a direct role owing to pressure caused by growth of the money stock, and an indirect role. In the medium- and long-term the increase in the money supply acts as an indicator and a lax instrument of monetary policy, influencing both internal inflationary expectations and speeding up transmission of international inflationary impulses.
Formally we obtain:

$$\Delta gp_t/gp_t = f\,(\Delta M_{t-1}/M_{t-1},\ \Delta p_{Mt-1}/p_{Mt-1}), \qquad [3.1]$$

where Δgp_{t-1} represents the rate of inflation, ΔM_{t-1} indicates the rate of growth of the money stock and $\Delta p_{Mt-1}/p_{Mt-1}$ the rate of increase of import prices (the delayed adjustment process of internal prices with respect to internal and external inflationary impulses). In the monetarist version the increase in money explains the excess demand in the goods market (and/or labour market) and the inclusion of import prices is wholly justified by their role in inflationary components, consisting of foreign exchange market tensions and difficulties in guaranteeing oil supplies (the second oil shock was as recent as 1979), whilst on the other price restraint (exacerbated by wage indexation mechanisms, the trend of labour costs and productivity) and marked sectorial difficulties in the production system constituted crucial internal issues.

In fact

> The right remedy for the trade cycle is not to be found in abolishing booms and thus keeping us permanently in a semi-slump; but in abolishing slumps and thus keeping us permanently in a quasi-boom. (Keynes, 1936, p. 322)

The booms (1976, 1979-80) were followed in more or less rapid succession by considerable external deficits which called for the restrictive action which triggered the subsequent recessions (1977 and 1981). The underlying peculiarity was that, unlike in the 1960s (1964 recession), the customary economic variables in the 1970s operated within a context of high inflation and a distressing output trend. The GDP gap materialised in the aftermath of the macro transformation of the economy during the three years between 1973 and 1975.

Substantial changes were observed in different sectors. The importance of the service sector became clear as it increased from 39% of GDP at constant prices in 1973 to 41% in 1980: this evidently confirmed the expansionary trend of this sector[2] within the economy. There was a slight improvement in the trend of industrial productivity despite a fall in the level of output. This was the result of a renewed climate of industrial relations, resulting in a reduction in the impact of the sliding scale, progress in the management of automatic wage adjustment mechanisms and a revival in investment. Massive recourse to *Cassa Integrazione*

---

dynamics in economic systems. For an application of the base rate of inflation to the Italian economy, cf. Fornasari (1984).

[2] The law of three sectors, or Colin Clark's Law, states that the percentage of employment and output in agriculture out of total employment and total production tend to decline, whilst the percentage of industry and the tertiary sector rise; cf. Clark (1940). In the version formulated by Sylos Labini (1983, pp. 83-4), the relative weight of the tertiary sector tends to grow as pro-capita income rises, even if this increase in not uniform in all countries.
In Italy - and in a simplistic view in which the tertiary sector is considered a homogeneous branch - such behaviour facilitates considerable absorption of manpower despite there is limited growth in productivity. The «backwardness» of this sector can be seen in the poor quality of supply and the power of inflationary thrusts. Cf. Barca and Visco (1993, pp. 69-81).

Guadagni (CIG, a government-funded temporary lay-off system)[3] aggravated state balances. The rate of inflation continued to rise, reaching a peak of 21.2%. The Italian economy was thus found itself on the verge of a vicious circle characterised by inflation, unemployment and falling output.

In 1981[4] appreciation of the US dollar and subsequent fluctuations in its

[3] Recourse to CIG (Dole and Welfare Benefits), often considered an automatic economic stabiliser, was increasingly frequent in the second half of the 1970s although whether it was indeed an automatic mechanism or not was highly debatable. This was also because the Bank of Italy was slow to realise that employment was an issue. Prior to 1984-85 the main targets for the Italian central bank were restraining inflationary restraint and a reduction in the rate of growth of the public debt.
Workers included in CIG might be considered equivalent to laid-off workers in other countries, the difference being that in Italy they were not included in unemployment figures. Thus whilst in Italy the consistent and continued use of this system did not raise concerns over the potential effects on unemployment levels, it did raise concerns over the size of the government deficit. In order to limit further deterioration of the deficit, as in other countries, attention focused on the potential importance of linking the proportion of unemployment benefit which employers were liable to pay to CIG workers to the frequency with which the firms resorted to CIG, in order to discourage abuse of the system.
Law 223 of 23 July 1991 complied with the dispositions set forth in Law 56 of 1987 and introduced innovations to labour market regulations and established new rules for CIG.

[4] 1981 was the first year of the Reagan administration. An essential element of *Reaganomics* (1981-82) was strong Supply Side Economics, the same line of thought that inspired *Thatcherism* in the United Kingdom from the end of the 1970s until the end of the 1980s.
Supply Side Economics involves reducing inflation without a slump, and a reduction in the tax burden is considered a necessary condition for a rapid increase in the rate of growth as well as being itself an instrument with which to increase tax revenue. It is however the radical fringe of this approach that has received greatest attention and is best known. The radical fringe emphasises the positive effects of lower tax on saving, investment, the supply of labour and at the same time tax revenue itself. The Laffer curve is enlightening, although somewhat disputed in its originality, since a version was formulated as early as the 14th century by Khaldûn (1967). The novelty of this approach may also be confuted by reference to the Physiocrats.
In fact the Mercantilists advocated heavy taxation above all on imports in order to subsidise exports. But the heavy tax burden and pronounced weakness of the French economy confirmed the success of the approach later put forward by the Physiocrats, who considered agriculture to be the only source of wealth so that both industry and commerce should be free from any form of tax. In theoretical

value coupled with high US interest rates[5] had a profound impact on the international outlook, with negative repercussions on the Italian economy which led to a decline in the level of employment[6] and thereby restricted potential for economic growth.

The decision by entrepreneurs to run down previously accumulated stocks of raw materials and semi-manufactured goods limited the trade deficit, despite a pronounced current account deficit in the face of the sizeable external outlays. Price rose significantly[7] and the lira weakened within the EMS, inducing the Italian authorities to introduce an interest-free loan on foreign payments (which remained in force until 1982). This made imports less profitable or at least encouraged entrepreneurs to seek extended payment terms, easing pressure on the exchange rate caused by the balance of payments deficit

Italian monetary policy became the mainstay of internal and external economic stability, in the absence of an appropriate budgetary policy. In order to guarantee a sufficient level of autonomy in order not to be conditioned in its policy choices, the Bank of Italy «divorced» from the Treasury and no longer committed itself to purchasing residual

---

terms Supply Side Economics is often associated with conservative political views, such as monetarism. However the economists from these groups where extremely critical of one another when trying to influence the Reagan administration. In terms of economic policy, supply-siders appear closer to the Keynesian approach than to monetarism for their proposals on tax breaks and expansionary monetary policy. On this approach cf. Fink (1982); Craig Roberts (1984). The rapid recovery witnessed in the United States between 1983 and 1984 would appear to confirm the opinions of the supply-siders, for whom incentives are essential factor for growth. An alternative explanation underlines the importance of the rapid increase in money stock and the expansion of the full employment government deficit. The two latter phenomena were confirmed empirically.

5 To counteract inflation in 1981 and 1982 the United States adopted strategies which had more in common with cold turkey than with gradualist measures.

6 Here it is important to understand that unlike other Western nations, in which a rise in the price of oil combined with converging internal factors modified the productive apparatus, Italy did not adequately protect the labour market. In the 1979s a number of policies were introduced to increase youth employment including the establishment of new industrial structures. In the 1980s attempts were made to increase employment in a number of sectors, whilst from 1984 onwards several strategies were devised to create new jobs, and at the same time a certain degree of deregulation in the labour market emerged.

7 In March 1981 the discount rate was increased from 16.5% to 19%. In the same year the reserve requirement mechanism was reviewed (Gambale, 1986, p. 275).

government bonds not taken up by the market.[8] The term «divorce» is perhaps rather too strong if taken literally. The Bank of Italy could not distance itself entirely from issues relating to state finance[9] and effectively such a decision implied that the Treasury was compelled to offer attractive yields in order to entice the general public to purchase bonds.

During the 1980s the anomalies in the fiscal and monetary regime which were later to leave their mark on the Italian economy emerged for the first time, and can essentially be summarised in four points: Italian public debt was very short-term, with frequent renewals; there was swift growth in the number of bonds held in household portfolios; real interest rates were high,

---

[8] This decision was taken in order to guarantee the independence of the central bank in monetary operations and did not indicate acceptance of monetarist rules, but rather reflected the clear limits imposed by the economic state of the country. Effectively the «divorce» (an institutional economic policy measure) was determined by the progressive accumulation of daily Treasury deficits which the Bank of Italy was obliged to cover, increasing the monetary base. The Treasury had clearly been undermined by the decision taken in the mid 1970s to centralise the daily borrowing requirement of the enlarged public sector taken in the mid 1970s. This explains the decision taken in 1981 to suppress the automatic and unlimited financing of the state by the Bank of Italy. The desire was to restore responsibility for ensuring that demand for bonds was adequate to cover funding requirements to the Treasury, thus offering the Bank of Italy the opportunity to regulate the monetary base according to its monetary control targets and the Government's general economic objectives. Such a division was justified on the grounds that responsibility for the control of liquidity was typically a part of monetary policy, and thus lay with the Bank of Italy. Public debt policies were responsible for financing the deficit with monetary base and renewing debt at maturity. Fiscal policy in Italy continued to exert an influence over monetary policy through the Treasury's current account, an account held at the Bank of Italy from which the Treasury was authorised to withdraw funds up to 14% of current public expenditure. The Treasury could withdraw funds at its discretion up to the set limit, so that the Bank of Italy was often forced to sterilise the monetary base. Nevertheless in 1993 the Treasury's automatic access to direct credit from the Bank of Italy was abolished.

[9] In January 1983 the Bank of Italy was forced to advance 8,000 billion lire to the Treasury for one year, since insufficient absorption of bonds by the market meant that the Treasury was no longer able to bring its current account overdraft back within legally imposed limits (14% of the revised state expenditure budget). Cf. Gambale (1986, p. 276). See also this author, among others, for an accurate summary of Italian economic trends from 1970 to 1985 contained in the appendix to his book. For an appraisal of the basic trends of the Italian economy see Valli (1993, *Parte Terza*).

despite the predominance of short-term, more liquid debt; crowding-out was not particularly significant (Vaciago, 1990, pp. 204-5).

In 1982 the inflationary process was apparently uncontrollable and heavily penalised the Italian economy in relation to other countries. The level of employment contracted in the absence of any signs of recovery in production. Interest rates rose and in an attempt to limit bank credit,[10] compulsory foreign currency loans were introduced for export credits (70% of the total amount). In June of the same year the lira was devalued by 2.75%. External demand declined, partially the result of the contraction of exports towards OPEC countries,[11] and internal demand followed suit. The result was a drop in the level of industrial capacity utilisation. A number of fiscal measures were introduced (a tax amnesty, increases in tax rates etc.) which however did nothing to ameliorate the deterioration in the accounts of the public sector, so that way the public sector borrowing requirement came to account for circa 17% of GDP.

The serious issues affecting the country's output structure clearly had an impact upon employment, and this vulnerability in turn created considerable difficulties for trade union organisations. In January 1983 the

[10] At the same time penalties applied to the banking system for exceeding limits imposed on the expansion of loans were made harsher.

[11] From 1981-82 the price of crude oil fell slightly for three reasons: (a) stagnating or even falling world demand for oil given the recession experienced by several countries required the urgent use of alternative sources of energy; (b) new exports reaching the crude oil markets, such as those from Mexico, Britain and Norway; (c) the political turmoil within OPEC which undermined its unity. In Italy the drop in the price of such a strategic raw material had a positive impact as early as 1982 with a reduction in the current account deficit of the balance of payments.

The OPEC crisis became came to the forefront between the second half of 1985 and March 1986, when the dollar price fell sharply (the oil counter-shock) and returned to levels observed before the 1979-80 energy crisis. At the same time the dollar exchange rate fell abruptly from September 1985 to March 1986, even against the lira. These events resulted in a considerable reduction in payments for imports of crude oil and a corresponding reduction in the oil deficit. Nevertheless this fall in the «oil bill» could have led to a drastic reduction in inflation or rapid economic expansion. The decision to almost totally absorb the benefits in taxation certainly improved *coeteris paribus* the public deficit but it limited the potential benefits to inflation and economic growth (Valli, 1990, p. 347).

It is also worth remembering Saudi Arabia's role as swing producer, increasing or decreasing production to maintain the total quotas constant. According to Beckerman (1985; 1986) it was precisely this fluctuation in raw material prices which favoured the drop in inflation and not the higher level of unemployment.

social partners (trade unions and *Confindustria* [the Confederation of Italian Industry]) with the government, signed a memorandum of agreement[12] over the definition of working hours and wage rises.[13] Nevertheless this attempt to restrain inflation to 13% by manipulating the cost of labour failed, since in the meantime public tariffs and the direct and indirect tax burden had increased significantly.

At the end of June 1983,[14] ceilings on bank credit were removed and at the end of the year interest rates rose,[15] making bonds easier to place on the

---

[12] In fact on 22 January 1983 with the «Scotti Agreement» between CGIL, CISL (the Italian Federation of Trade Unions), UIL (the Italian Trade Unions Confederation), the Government and *Confindustria* a range of measures were adopted to limit the automatic adjustment of wages, by setting a new value for the allowance point and excluding certain elements from the calculation. The value of the allowance point became the same for all categories of workers, but the degree of coverage of wages in the sliding scale was reduced by 10% (from circa 73% to 63%)

[13] «The first point of the agreement concerning a total reduction of 40 hours by 1985 has been respected in the main sectors of industry with a staggered reduction in working hours in the second half of 1984 and the first part of 1985. Compliance with limits imposed on wages increases, of 25, 35 and 40 thousand lire per month for the three year period 1983-1985 is more difficult to assess since significant differences have emerged between different sectors. If we consider the largest sector, it is estimated that public and private employees in the metal and mechanical industry received increases in excess of agreed amounts in 1983, as a result of one-off payments which more than compensated the delays in signing the national employment contracts. Wage increases for employees in the chemical, textile and food sectors were within limits. In all sectors differentiation of wage increases between categories of workers was observed, evidence of the will to reconsider wage differentials which had been continuously eroded by the workings of the sliding scale with a uniform allowance point» (Banca d'Italia, 1984, *Relazione Economica*, p. 98)

[14] As we have already seen, the Italian monetary authorities preferred TDC as their intermediate target, with a few lapses from 1974 to 1983. TDC lost significance as a result of the inadequate degree of control afforded by monetary intervention in the light of the institutional situation and TDC's decreased relevance with the final target.
For a wide-ranging analysis of Bank of Italy intervention, see Bertocco (1991); and for an examination of the performance of the Governors of numerous central banks see Ciocca (1983).

[15] Nominal interest rates on government bonds from 1979 to 1983 were in excess of 14% and reached 20% in 1982. These levels triggered a drop in the ratio of bank deposits to GDP, giving rise to the phenomenon of credit disintermediation. This ratio was bound to fall in view of the growing use of

market. This restrained the creation of the monetary base and offered an opportunity to repay (the following January) the Bank of Italy's Lombard loan to the Treasury. Economic policy priorities focused on re-establishing macroeconomic equilibria with a resulting squeeze on consumption and investment.

At the end of September 1983 the Government presented its economic policy for 1984, asserting that monetary stability and recovery of output were complementary objectives to be pursued simultaneously. This dual target could only be achieved by means of a more balanced budgetary policy, supported by substantial corrective measures focusing on revenue and expenditure, and bolstered by action to slow down the rate of increase of nominal wages in order to dampen menacing price-wage spirals.

The M2 monetary aggregate[16] surpassed TDC in 1984, acquiring specific value for monetary policy targets and becoming an important transmission mechanism of the effects of monetary intervention. In the 1980s it became virtually impossible for the Bank of Italy to maintain TDC as a target; since growth in the internal borrowing requirement of the state sector[17] would have made it necessary to sacrifice credit to firms to below the natural level required for production to continue.

alternative systems of payment, such as credit cards, and the strong competition from other new payment methods. Credit disintermediation demonstrated how a growing proportion of saving was invested with final borrowers.

[16] In the Appendix to the numerous Annual Reports, the Bank of Italy provides the current definitions of money in relation to the different degree of liquidity of financial assets. M1 is money comprising the so-called primary liquidity, i.e. bank notes, coins, bank and post office sight deposits and sight deposits at the Treasury. M2 is M1 plus secondary liquidity, comprising bank and post office saving deposits, spot against forward bank deposits and bank certificates of deposit. If the latter are removed from M2 we obtain M2A. Extended M2 includes, in addition to all the components of M2, bank deposits of Italian residents at overseas branches of Italian banks. M3, the aggregate that was adopted until 1991 is M2 plus treasury bills and banker's acceptances. The Bank of Italy preferred to focus on M2 since sight deposits bear interest and are not clearly distinct from savings deposits. It follows that the distinction between M1 and M2 is not of great relevance. The definition given in Italy to M2 corresponds to the definition of M3 harmonised at the EU level (often indicated by the acronym EC).
Total liquid assets in addition to M2 include banker's acceptances, special credit institute certificates of deposit, spot against forward securities, interest-bearing post office deposits and short term government debt.

[17] The public sector borrowing requirement is estimated by the CIP, which is also responsible for examining and approving the planned growth of the non-state sector and of the money stock notified by the Governor of the Central Bank.

At the start of 1984 the situation appeared slightly less oppressive, with a marked improvement in the balance of payments. It was a year of tangible economic recovery both in Italy and internationally. In February attempts were made to reach an agreement to limit the sliding scale by offering a series of tax incentives and more favourable employment policies. However in the face of opposition from CGIL, the Government imposed a decree (the St. Valentine's decree of 14 February 1984) introducing controls on wages and public tariffs, as well as controlled prices. The referendum demanded by the opposition to repeal the law and restore the urtailed allowance points lost did nothing to alter this situation,[18] indeed *Confindustria* immediately announced the definite suspension of the sliding scale. Tensions between the two opposing factions eased only in 1985 following the settlement on the sliding scale for civil servants, which was later extended to workers in the private sector.

Labour productivity increased significantly, and with it increases in the cost of labour eased. Combined with acceptable rises in public tariffs and controlled prices, this led to a mere 10% growth in prices, which represented the overriding policy target at the time. Nonetheless the lira depreciated with respect to the dollar. Despite price moderation, export growth was insufficient to compensate for the growth in imports, and generated a current account deficit in the balance of payments.

GDP growth was accompanied by significant expansion of bank credit following the abolition of credit ceilings.[19] Restrictive monetary policy was

[18] It seems likely that the Government's announcement of the target for inflation and the reduction in the allowance point applied to the sliding scale brought beneficial effects, with a more rapid downward shift of the hypothetical Phillips curve, which limited the loss of income caused by disinflation. On this theme cf. Guiso and Magnani (1985), and Gressani, Guiso and Visco (1988).

[19] Ceilings on bank loans of various percentages were removed in 1983, introduced again in the first half of 1986 and once again imposed between September 1987 and March 1988. The Italian experience demonstrates that on the one hand ceilings only partially affect the financing of production, since operations in foreign currency are allowed, whilst on the other it strengthens controls using traditional methods. «The above mentioned ceiling diverted the supply of bank credit which could not be offered as loans towards foreign bonds, with the effect of limiting the creation of monetary base via internal channels and reducing yields on treasury bills in relation to those on bank loans. In addition the application of the ceilings exclusively to loans in lire induced the banks to increase net foreign debts in order to satisfy the demand for foreign currency loans. The latter were not subject to quotas and thus partially replaced loans in lire, the cost of which was pushed up by the scarcity of supply»

introduced as a result, consisting of renewed portfolio restrictions for lending banks and a ban on increases in net external debts over and above the level reached at the end of June. The discount rate was raised to 16.5%.[20] In an attempt to contain the burden of interest on state balances a law was passed at the end of the year introducing a unified treasury for state agencies.

The moderate rate of price growth and the application of fiscal measures brought the interest rate down to 15.5% at the beginning of 1985. At the same time mandatory foreign currency loans for exports invoiced in foreign currency falling due within one year from customs clearance were halved.

The recovery which commenced in 1984 continued into the following year although in 1985 the difficulties created by public finance became even more pressing. Economic growth was stimulated by internal demand so that internal absorption at what were considered profitable prices significantly crowded out the propensity to supply overseas markets. This generated a deficit in the current account of the balance of payments. In order to gain ground in international markets, in July 1985 in the aftermath of the sensational rise in the dollar which continued until the end of September, the lira was devalued by 6% within the EMS. In October mandatory foreign currency loans for exports with deferred collection were abolished, and the interest rate fell to 15%.

(Predetti, 1990, p. 91). This resulted in greater flexibility of credit control, above all in favour of the firms most actively engaged in foreign trade. The abolition of the ceilings induced the monetary authorities to focus intervention on open market operations and the reserve requirement.

[20] In the first half of 1984 an attempt was made to promote a new approach in the market for treasury bills, given that the Bank of Italy's participation in the auction was finalised towards monetary control and that following the «divorce» it no longer guaranteed coverage of the public sector borrowing requirement. In order to strengthen and stabilise the demand for new treasury bills a pool of major banks guaranteed to take up the entire issue of treasury bills at each auction for an agreed amount. The Bank of Italy in turn agreed to finance in the very short term a part of the issue taken up by institutions belonging to the pool in order to assure the pool greater funding: if yields on treasury bills were not sufficiently attractive in theory this would have created tension within the pool, given that banks participated on a voluntary basis. Long term disequilibrium would have implied growth in banks' own bond portfolios, which would in turn have led the whole agreement to be abandoned.

The substantial devaluation of the dollar[21] and the drop in oil prices did not however have a significant influence upon the Italian economy, and did not produce the desired fall in prices. It became apparent that an unwanted and unyielding element existed, termed core inflation to underline the existence of an inflationary base (estimated at the time at around 8-9%) which was hard to repress and which was fuelled by the increasing imbalance in public finance[22] and by brisk growth in real interest rates.

1986 was an important year in which the economy reaped the rewards of carefully directed policies to protect the economy from destabilising imbalances, were reaped, combined with the positive impact of the upward cyclical trend. The intricate issues of the previous 15 years began unravel. Production and internal demand accelerated, by 2.7% and 3.2% respectively. The trade deficit improved as a result of the improved terms of trade, and the current account of the balance of payments recorded a surplus. Encouraged by attractive profit margins, firms invested in plant and machinery. The public sector borrowing requirement was contained within the 1985 level of 110,000 billion lire.[23] Retail price increases were modest, and there was significant downward pressure on inflation, which fell to an average annual rate of 5.9%. Italy's negative inflation differential compared to other nations declined considerably.

The downturn in inflation coincided with the recovery of enterprise. These two processes were determined by common, interacting factors. Undoubtedly growth was boosted by the recovery of productivity thanks to the introduction of new technology, innovations in production and

---

[21] The limited devaluation of the US dollar led to expectations of a realignment of exchange rate parities within the EMS. Such expectations induced foreign agents to decrease their foreign currency debts and increase their credits. The result was a considerable loss of foreign exchange reserves.

[22] In the first quarter of 1985 monetary expansion accelerated under pressure from the state sector borrowing requirement. Bond issues was not being fully taken up as a result of unattractive yields, and so the Treasury was forced to use its account at the Bank of Italy thereby creating monetary base. There were peculiar consequences for state finance: any increase in the inflation rate recorded between the calculation of tax returns and their actual payment eroded the real value of such returns. This phenomenon came to be defined the «Olivera-Tanzi effect» despite already having been identified by Bresciani Turroni (1931; 1978). See also Olivera (1967) and Tanzi (1977).

[23] The public sector borrowing requirement net of interest payments and repayment of debt relating to previous periods fell from 47,000 to 36,000 billion lire (Banca d'Italia, 1987, *Considerazioni Finali*, p. 11).

different combinations of available resources. This eased pressure on unit costs and slowed price growth.

Although the year 1986 marked the end of a long period of deflation,[24] this was principally to be ascribed to the fall of the dollar and a decrease in energy costs. However as we have already mentioned it is important not to underestimate efforts by central authorities and social partners to correct existing imbalances. A significant role was played by the sliding scale. However not all issues were solved: the state deficit remained of vast proportions, firms were still not investing sufficiently to expand production, and the economic recovery was inadequate. The rate of unemployment rose to 11.1%, and the discount rate was lifted in several steps to 12%. From an long-term viewpoint,

> 1986 conflicts with the general hypothesis of an elastic global demand function with respect to the average price level: the supply "counter-shock" deriving from the dramatic fall in oil prices and the decline in international prices of other primary products was followed by a slowdown in inflation and not by more rapid income and employment growth in the industrial economies. (Ciocca, 1987, p. 103)

The year 1987 commenced with a liquidity squeeze in order to curb the outflow of reserves which had started in 1986. After the currency realignment of 11 January considerable monetary inflows were recorded, partly the result of the weakness of the dollar. The effects of such inflows were only partially neutralised by open market operations. Great concern was expressed over the expansion of foreign currency loans, made more attractive by the interest rate differential. The authorities intervened in mid March and imposed a reserve requirement on banks' overseas deposits. The aim was to limit growth of the overseas element of bank credit on the one hand and to increase the efficiency of indirect forms of control on the other. The expansion of the public sector borrowing requirement and the low propensity to invest in bonds were coupled with a corresponding rise in liquidity. The Bank of Italy retaliated with restrictive policies and raised

[24] On the causes of Italian disinflation in the 1980s cf. Giavazzi and Spaventa (1989). Balducci, Candela and Scorcu (2001, p. 409) estimate the sacrifice ratio at 1.4% p.a. of excess unemployment for a 1% reduction in the rate of inflation. For a different approach to the estimate which takes the cumulative rise in unemployment as the numerator rather than the sum of annual percentage points of excess unemployment (so that from 1980 to 1986 the figure for Italy was 5%) see Dawson (1992). For specific analysis of the sacrifice ratio, see Ball (1994, pp. 155-93).

interest rates.[25] The non-interest-bearing loan on overseas investments was abolished in mid May, which led to readjustment of private portfolios. In the summer the allocation of the treasury bills tender was successful in view of the rise in yields, whilst expectations of a currency devaluation led to significant losses in exchange reserves for the Bank of Italy. Downward pressure on the lira called for measures to limit short-term capital movements linked to foreign trade flows. A ceiling was imposed on the expansion of bank credit and the reserve requirement coefficient on foreign deposits was reduced to zero.

The results achieved in 1987 were generally satisfactory. Real income and output increased, the volume of investments in plant and machinery rose and retail prices fell to an average annual growth rate of 4.7%, the lowest level since 1969, following a slight decline in the price of imports coupled with the weakness of the dollar. In the manufacturing sector the cost-push wage effect was absent and in the labour market in general there was less recourse to CIG. Interest rate adjustments were less frequent in 1987 than in the previous year, although the discount rate was once again raised to 12% after falling to 11.5%. Exchange rate pressure and the conviction that measures to counteract the business cycle would prove ineffective led once more to the introduction of currency restrictions and specific guidelines for bank loans in lire.[26]

Creeping inflation, buoyant internal demand, deterioration of foreign accounts and feeble demand for government bonds were all understandably perceived as disturbing variables, despite a fall in raw material prices and the downward trend in CLUP which had positive effects on inflation rate dynamics. In this complex scenario consolidation of the public deficit emerged quite clearly as the paramount problem of the

[25] The real interest rate trend was curious. In the 1970s real interest rates were below nominal rates whilst in the 1980s the opposite was true. On the social implications of high interest rates, cf. Pasinetti (1996). See also Pasinetti (2000) for an analysis of the sustainability of public finance in Europe and for a link with the financial markets cf. Vaciago (1990).

[26] In the Unites States the situation in the stock market induced the chairman of the Federal Reserve Board Alan Greenspan to reduce interest rates thereby providing the necessary liquidity to stave off the risk of a crash. Effectively he applied the Bagehot principle (Bagehot, 1986), whereby the role of the central bank is crucial as lender of last resort. In this role it ultimately guarantees the solvency of the banking system, which in turn is responsible for creating a climate of trust in dealings with monetary institutions. This principle was totally disregarded in 1929 as Friedman and Schwartz (1963; 1965) highlight.

Italian economy, not only in terms of its effects upon the business cycle but also in view of its long-term implications.

Widespread optimism at the start of 1988[27] over the prospect of maintaining or increasing internal demand contrasted with the justified fear that the ongoing process of expansion might end. Growth in output was indeed driven by internal demand, which as it grew posed a threat to the fragile balance of the Italian economy. Buoyant internal demand led to rapid growth in imports, whilst Italian sales in foreign markets grew proportionately less. There was however a significant improvement in the energy balance. Net inward capital flows (close to 10 billion lire, twice the level of the previous year) helped the lira to hold up in the foreign exchange market. However the growing rate of inflation meant that the country's productive apparatus was not sufficiently competitive in international markets. The resurgence of inflation was explained by an increase in the rate of VAT, an increase in the lira-dollar exchange rate, wage growth in certain sectors and persistent excess liquidity. The decision taken in August 1988 to raise the discount rate triggered other interest rate changes.

In 1989 uncertainty over the future of public finance influenced the stock exchange and the decisions of savers. The government's fiscal measures, the so-called «stangata espansiva» (expansionary squeeze) disorientated medium- and long-term financial investments. Rising demand and certain potentially inflationary components (such as the drought) fuelled prices. Inflation rose (to 6.3% in February) and caused further switching of private resources towards consumption. The increase in the discount rate announced at the beginning of March was justified by conditions in the monetary and financial markets but created serious problems for private investment. In such intricate circumstances the risk of a vicious circle fuelled by rising demand and rising prices called for the urgent readjustment of public finance to abate tension in the markets: at the time it was forecasted that in 1992 public debt would reach 120% of

[27] In 1988 complete liberalisation of capital movements (Spain, Greece and Portugal followed in 1992) and the lira's entry into the EMS narrow fluctuation band (January 1990) were concrete steps towards the process of real and financial integration and monetary unification within the EC. On this subject see Basevi, Ferrari, Onofri and Poli (1993). Italy's entry into the EMS narrow fluctuation band was sought by the central bank, convinced that with foreign prices taken as given, the exchange rate determines internal prices. The central bank was also convinced that social partners and Government authorities would check their inflationary behaviour for fear of decreasing competitiveness. See Jossa and Musella (1996, pp. 101-4).

GDP. In March 1989 a policy to introduce the automatic indexation of income brackets from the following year was approved.

The dynamics of Italian industry,[28] which grew considerably during the 1980s, became the subject of a heated debate, particularly in terms of the performance of the industrial structure.[29] Nevertheless

[28] For an appraisal of the Italian industrial sector cf., Cipolletta (1986; 1990), Prosperetti (1993) and Onida (1993) among others. It should be remembered that the developments in the internal productive apparatus which began in the seventies and continued in the eighties and nineties confirmed two extraordinary events: «The first was a change in the dimension of industry: large firms greatly declined in importance and made way for smaller enterprises, which were less inhibited in their management of the workforce and in adapting to fluctuations in demand. The second was the increasingly widespread entry of foreign capital into Italian industry» (Graziani, 1997, p. 10).

[29] The push towards deregulation (a line of economic policy associated with conservative governments such as those of Reagan and Thatcher) and above all the state of emergency arising from the disarray in public finance focused attention on denationalization and transformation of Italian public corporations. In the 1985 *Relazione previsionale e programmatica* (Economic Policy Document) presented by the Finance Minister Goria the need to privatise industry was underlined, advocating a decrease in the role of the state and an increase in the role of the market. Progress towards the achievement of this objective was made by the Amato government between 1992 and 1993. Nevertheless fears of creating conditions conducive to the formation of a monopoly resulted in detailed anti-trust legislation in 1990. The *Autorità Garante della Concorrenza* (Competition Authority) was established to regulate the activity of public and private firms.
Experience in other countries demonstrated that privatization could be achieved in a number of ways. The choice was not easy considering the potential impact on the financial world and the crucial changes that would result in the relationship between citizens, firms and the state. At an international level four principal forms of privatization were identified. The transfer of control to a strategic buyer would imply sale of the company to be privatised to a sole purchaser who would then takes control. This path was chosen for small companies or those in serious economic difficulty (such as the purchase of Alfa Romeo by FIAT). The strategic buyer focuses on the long-term investment and tries to create operational synergies. In Italy minority stakes have often been listed on the stock exchange (for example this approach was adopted by IRI (the Italian Institute for Industrial Reconstruction) in the privatization of STET (the Turin Telephone Company). In this case control is retained by the majority shareholder. The creation of a hard core combined with listing on the stock exchange would imply sale of a minority stake to one or more strategic buyers operating in partnership and sale of the remaining shares on the stock exchange (as in the case of Argentina and Mexico). Complete privatization on the stock

> Recent data on the other hand highlights how in the second half of the eighties the profitability of small and medium sized enterprises declined significantly; how the market share of Italian exports appeared to be contracting; and finally how several large enterprises were showing signs of strain. (Prosperetti, 1993, p. 128)

In terms of monetary policy, between 1988 and 1989 there was a clear preference for restrictive measures which led the target of exchange rate stability to be abandoned, paving the way for the appreciation of the lira within the EMS.

3.2 The controversial start of the nineties

The year 1990 was marked by three important events on the world stage: the new political balance in Eastern Europe[30] culminating in a united Germany;[31] the Gulf Crisis[32] culminating in Desert Storm on 17 January of the following year and the economic downswing which was more severe than expected.

Undoubtedly the new economic and political outlook in the wake of German reunification and above all the new perspective in Central and Eastern Europe called for the redefinition of Europe albeit at an appropriate pace.

---

exchange could be performed in two ways. In the first case, which is typical in the Anglo-Saxon world, 100% of the share capital is offered concurrently on the internal and on international stock exchanges. The second case differs in that the state retains a so-called golden share for a limited or an unlimited period of time in order to influence the strategy of the denationalised company.

[30] The East European countries proceeded with the complex transition from planned economies to market economies as a natural consequence of the political events and above all the fall of the Berlin Wall in November 1989. Economic and productive reorganisation combined with shortages in raw materials and brisk inflation provoked by so-called "shortageflation" caused a considerably weakened of production in many countries. On this peculiar aspect of the inflationary process see, among others, Kornai (1980; 1982); Kolodko and McMahon (1987).

[31] Germany came to experience a situation which resembled the Italian situation, with an economic gap clearly dividing the nation in two.

[32] For an analysis of the impact of the Gulf Crisis on economic systems in general and on the Italian economy in particular see Clò (1992).

The Gulf War added 0.5% to the rate of inflation which reached 6.5%[33] in Italy and sparked negative expectations concerning the business cycle. The stability of the lira within the EMS, which was the priority of monetary policy, and the weakness of the dollar combined to contain growth in import prices. However the public deficit[34] was still of alarming proportions[35] and indeed in 1990 public debt surpassed annual GDP.[36] In the same year real GDP growth was 2% compared to 3% the previous year. Gross fixed investment rose by 3% and in particular the revival in purchases of plant and machinery and in construction boosted internal demand, which was suffering the effects of the Gulf War. Private and

---

[33] The persistence of the differential between retail prices and producer prices was principally justified by the rigidity of brokerage margins, the increase in public tariffs required to restrain the state deficits as well as the effects of the expected increases in indirect taxation.

[34] The problem was remarkable and inspired a number of contributions. The of «Barro-Ricardo equivalence» underlines how financing expenditure by issuing public debt is equivalent to financing the debt through current taxation. See Ricardo (1954) and also Barro (1974). The efficacy of measures on expenditure financed by public debt rather than by increasing money is that it would increase disposable income, thereby amplifying the expansionary effects of public expenditure at least in the long-term, and give rise to the «Blinder-Solow paradox» (Blinder and Solow, 1973; 1974). This result would be neutralised out by a deficit reducing policy, as increased taxation would compensate the increase in disposable income generated by interest payments. In the model formulated by Sargent and Wallace (1981) fiscal policy dominates monetary policy, a situation which the authors identify more frequently in real life. They demonstrate that if a public deficit occurs, the choice of restrictive monetary policy may create more inflation in the long run than an expansionary monetary policy. For an analysis of the various approaches concerning the effects of financing expenditure with government bonds see Stevenson, Muscatelli and Gregory (1988, paragraph 6.3).

[35] The target of rebalancing state finance went off course for a number of reasons: the trend of interest expenses, the renewal of a series of public sector labour contracts concentrated over a short space of time, and growth in tax revenue which fell short of expectations. In this scenario, also considering the Maastricht Agreement, an explanation about a possible war of attrition cannot exist, cf. Alesina and Drazen (1991).

[36] From 1975 to 1990 the sizeable burden of interest payments was added to the growing public debt. Throughout this period interest rates never fell below 10%, with peaks between 1981 and 1992. Current government expenditure "financed" the payment of interest on previously issued bonds. Undoubtedly the fall in interest rates which began in 1995 contributed to bring the level of government debt back under control.

collective consumption also surged. In these renewed circumstances a slight fall in the propensity to save was recorded, from 20% to 19.3% of GDP.[37]

Nevertheless we should be aware that

> Between 1971 and 1990 productivity in Italian manufacturing industry grew at an average rate of 4.4% p.a.. This average is a combination of very diverse trends and factors during the various stages of the trade cycle and the process of industrial reconstruction. Over the twenty year period the average rate of productivity growth exceeded the corresponding rates of growth of German and French industry by 2% and 15% respectively. (Banca d'Italia, 1992, *Considerazioni Finali*, p. 20)

The creeping transmission of the cost-push effect on prices, delays in the sliding scale, the timing of the introduction of certain tariff and fiscal measures slowed both the acceleration and deceleration of prices in the aftermath of the outbreak and the conclusion of the Gulf War. Certain peculiarly Italian anomalies could not fail to emerge. Indeed,

> Whilst we expect high unemployment rates to be associated with an external surplus and low unemployment rates to be associated with a deficit, in the Italian economy, and not only the Italian economy, it seems that a high rate of unemployment [...] went hand in hand with growing deficits on the current account of the balance of payments, an indication of the considerable structural imbalances in the Italian economy, and not just the Italian

[37] In this context the Neisser effect springs to mind. If economic growth is the result of population increase, younger households with a higher propensity to save constitute a greater proportion of the population than in a stationary economy. Thus the positive saving of the working age population is higher than the negative saving of the elderly and the national rate of saving is positive. In the Italian economy, characterised by a shrinking population, this effect may offer a key to the interpretation of the slump in saving. See also Casarosa (1991, p. 409).
The life cycle model underlines how saving by the elderly is negative. See Ando and Kennickel (1986). On the subject of saving, Guiso, Jappelli and Terlizzese (1992) reveal how the relationship between economic growth and imperfections in the capital market can explain the high level of Italian saving as well as its gradual decline. In fact an economy in which families are subject to liquidity restrictions generally has higher rates of saving than an economy with more efficient financial markets, even if both grow at the same rate. Additionally the fall in the rate of growth in the two countries will lead to a proportionately higher fall in the rate of saving in the country with the imperfect capital market.

economy (in Japan there seem to be exactly the opposite imbalances!). (Marzano, 1991, p. 273)

The protracted American recession which lasted longer than expected, the end of the expansion in Germany and Japan,[38] as well as the economic and monetary disintegration in Central and Eastern Europe sparked tensions which exacerbated the downswing in the industrialised countries. In 1991 Italy was faced not only with problems related to the international recession, but also with unsatisfactory economic policy management, excessive growth in labour costs, insufficient initiative by enterprise and the increasingly alarming state of public finance. These imbalances posed a threat to the country's output structure, and also to its long-term development, and thus risked excluding Italy from the path laid down in the Maastricht Agreement.

In 1991 the fall in the level of economic activity[39] was initially interpreted as a crisis in the confidence of consumers[40] and enterprises following the Gulf War. Later forecasts focused on the positive impact of the successful conclusion to the war, which precluded a permanent increase in the price of oil. Thus recovery was expected to resemble the experience of the 1980s, the aftermath of the recession which followed the second oil shock. Contrary to all expectations, the initial downswing degenerated into a full-blown recession.[41]

[38] The Japanese recession of the 1990s had much in common with the Great Depression, despite being quite distinct. In both cases share prices fell, real estate prices dwindled, there was a banking crisis, low interest rates and a fall in consumption coupled with lively debate over the growth of public debt and a possible increase of the money supply.

[39] During the general recession of 1991-93, inventories increased much less than in the 1981-83 recession. This can probably be explained by the part-in-time management techniques imported from Japan involving synchronisation between suppliers and users of materials.

[40] In the Unites States the consumer confidence index explained the national recession from 1991 to 1992 which then sent into reverse gear the international economy. Consumers reduced expenditure on consumption although income remained constant.

[41] The recession appeared to be less serious for the major industrial economies than the recessions following the two oil shocks, with the exception of the United Kingdom and Canada. The lesser intensity was due to both the absence of sudden supply shocks and the lack of synchronisation between the various countries. However the duration of this downswing was superior to the previous average. For a comparison of previous cycles experienced in the major countries cf. Caselli (1992).

In 1991 retail price inflation fluctuated around an annual average 6.4%, roughly twice the level of the other countries in the narrow EMS exchange rate band. The unemployment rate fell slightly from 11% in 1990 to 10.9%.[42] Fortunately the cost of imports fell in view of the stability of the lira and the reasonable prices of raw materials and energy. This meant that inflationary impulses were entirely the result of internal origin.[43]

In order to facilitate comparison and foster co-ordination between nations, the monetary aggregate M2[44] was adopted as a monetary target and was calculated in terms of quarterly averages. Banks were required to reduce loans but to support the real economy (Banca d'Italia, 1992, *Considerazioni Finali*, p. 14).

---

[42] In 1989 the average value of this indicator was, for the third year in succession, 12%. Naturally unemployment varied according to age, sex and residence. The labour market thus came to resemble that described in the hysteresis model. Nonetheless empirical studies offered surprising results. The analysis conducted by Bodo and Visco (1987) while critical of the interpretative capacity of the model, underlines how unemployment was caused by structural motives, including the discrepancy between the availability of professional skills and the needs of entrepreneurs (Padoa Schioppa F., 1990). Bodo and Visco (1987) however do not consider that hysteresis may be due to the regional distribution of unemployment. In this revised approach, unemployed labour from the South would have a limited influence on wage dynamics, which are substantially dependent on labour market conditions in the Centre-North. Following this analytical approach Bodo and Sestito (1989) reveal how hysteresis was a feature peculiar to the Italian labour market on a regional basis.
For detailed analysis of hysteresis and eurosclerosis, which characterise the European labour market and render it much less flexible than its American counterpart, cf. Chrystal, Faini and Guiso (1991, pp. 202-7), while for an analysis of the labour market in Italy and comparison at an EU (European Union) level see Dell'Aringa (1993).

[43] In this context note that «The abolition of the reserve requirement on banks' net overseas foreign currency deposits limited the flow of loans granted by overseas branches of Italian banks. In addition the inclusion of state operations in portfolio investments reduced net revenue by 5,000 billion lire compared to 1990. Overall there was a momentuous contraction of overseas loans (from 36,200 to 13,400 billion lire)» Banca d'Italia (1992, *Relazione Economica*, p. 126).

[44] In the new definition spot against forward operations between banks and customers and interest-bearing post-office deposits were not included, while the so-called extended M2 included M2 plus deposits at overseas branches of Italian banks. For a continuous update on the definitions of liquid assets including the euro-area, see the most recent issue of the Bank of Italy's Annual Report.

Towards the end of 1991, the increasing discrepancy between monetary conditions in Germany and the United States[45] led to tension in currency markets which also involved the lira. In the second half of December Germany raised its discount rate and the United States lowered it,[46] and interest rates subsequently edged up in almost all European countries: in Italy rates rose by 0.5% to 12%.

Overall results in macroeconomic terms for 1992[47] were a 0.9% deceleration of growth in GDP, an average annual rate of inflation of 5.3%, and a balance of payments current account deficit which rose to 2.2% of GDP (Banca d'Italia, 1993, *Considerazioni Finali*, p. 11). Public debt rose to from 1,318,244 billion lire at the end of 1990 to 1,485,141 billion lire in December 1991 and to 1,673,574 billion lire in December 1992. As a proportion of GDP public debt increased from 100.5% in 1990 to 104.1% in 1991 reaching 110.0% in 1992 (*Ibid.*, *Relazione Economica*, p. 134). Thus the crucial role of the "credibility factor" in conditioning the dynamics of currency and financial variables, and hence economic policy itself, became apparent.[48]

In the same year the monetary aggregate became exceptionally important in view of the Government's virtually simultaneous

[45] The announcement on 12 August 1992 of the signing of the agreement between the USA, Mexico and Canada marked the start of the North Atlantic Free Trade Agreement (NAFTA). In the first half of August 1993 a number of collateral elements concerning environmental protection and the protection of the rights of workers were added. The general NAFTA was approved by US Congress on 18 November 1993 despite strong opposition.

[46] The change in US leadership, officially with effect from the start of 1993 was radical. After 12 years of an approach founded upon moderate fiscal burdens, regressive taxation, the absence of state intervention in the economy and continued expansion of the state deficit, Bill Clinton inaugurated his so-called *Clintonomics* by passing a programme which increased the tax burden, re-instated a form of progressiveness in the tax system, expanded public investment in a number of sectors and at the same time aimed to reduce the public deficit. As the President himself announced, investment growth and reduction of the public deficit were objectives that had never previously been pursued.

[47] In February 1992 the Bank of Italy took on responsibility for fixing the discount rate and the rate on Lombard loans (a role previously assigned to the Treasury Minister who evaluated proposals from the Governor).

[48] On this subject cf. Alesina, Cohen and Roubini (1997).

announcement of a series of restrictive measures.[49] This demonstrated finely the tuned intentions of the authorities responsible for monetary and fiscal policy[50] were finely tuned, although there was mutual recognition of their respective fields of action. As a result the markets regained confidence. However the performance of industrial enterprises confirmed the fragility of the Italian productive apparatus, and any hopes of recovery were dashed by the sudden increase in the cost of money occasioned by the rise in interest rates.[51]

The weakening of the lira within the EMS[52] induced the Bank of Italy to raise the discount rate at the beginning of July. Speculative movements against the lira prompted policy makers to increase the discount rate from 12% to 13%, and later to 15% on 4 September 1992. This rise in interest rates augmented an increase in the interest burden, not only for firms but also for the state sector in servicing the public debt. With the aid of

[49] A number of strategies pursued by the Amato Government focused upon health, pensions and local finance culminating in the restrictive manoeuvre of summer 1992.
The budget manoeuvre was achieved through increased fiscal revenues, an agreement on the cost of labour (in which the abolition of the sliding scale played a fundamental role), the disposal of buildings and other state properties, the liquidation of the EFIM, and the conversion of IRI, ENI (the National Hydrocarbon Corporation), INA (the National Insurance Institute), ENEL, and *Ferrovie dello Stato* (the National Railways Company) into joint-stock companies as part of a massive privatization programme. In 1993 a local property tax (ICI) was introduced.
In that year the fluctuation bands within the EMS, which Italy had abandoned the year before, were increased to ± 15%.

[50] In 1992 an extraordinary property tax was levied (ISI) and was replaced the following year by ICI.

[51] In June 1993 following a proposal from the Bank of Italy, the CICR authorised banks, in certain circumstances, to provide capital for firms.

[52] The Italian lira exited the EMS on 17 September 1992. From 1992 to 1993 following the European exchange rate crisis, the Italian lira and the British pound devalued by 10% and 15% respectively. Both in Britain and in Italy the trade balance was negative and the rate of growth of income was extremely low. The devaluation benefited Italy, unlike Britain. Following liberalisation of capital movements and the creation of the single market, achieved before the establishment of the European Central Bank (ECB), national monetary policies exercised a lower level of regulatory power which was not compensated by an increase at a community level. The fact that the EMS substantially operated until 1992, and the convergence of macroeconomic policy, is to be attributed to the fluctuation bands which allowed a considerable degree of variation and permitted may countries to adopt systems to control capital flows.

government mediation, a settlement was finally reached between social partners at the end of July. The consequent re-stabilisation of wage dynamics between the public and private sectors and the abolition of the sliding scale resulted in moderate wage increases, with beneficial effects upon international competitiveness.

The slowdown in inflation continued into the early months of the following year,[53] thanks to the stance of monetary policy, the weakness of internal demand, the fall in the foreign currency price of imported goods and wage restraint.[54] Undoubtedly in limiting inflationary dynamics the refusal of social partners to rely on the wage-price spiral to protect labour income was a decisive factor (Banca d'Italia, 1993, *Considerazioni Finali*, p. 17).

During the course of 1993[55] the Italian lira[56] depreciated by 7%, benefiting exports which had already risen sharply at the end of 1992.[57] However this strong export growth was not sufficient, in 1993 at least, to stave off the decline in internal demand and boost production above the level recorded at the end of the previous year. The prospect of growing

[53] In November 1993 the Bank of Italy was authorised to set the reserve requirement within a limit of 17.5% of deposits. From that moment both compulsory Lombard loans on the Treasury account and the legal right to extraordinary Lombard loans were revoked by an Act of Parliament in compliance with the Maastricht Agreement.

[54] From 1 January 1993, with the completion of the single European market and the abolition of customs at internal borders, trade between member states was recorded by the Intrastat Statistical System. The system is based directly on declarations made by the firms involved, for fiscal and statistical purposes. Firms with exports or imports in excess of 150 million lire p.a. are liable to submit the declarations, which replace former customs documents. The latter remain compulsory for non-EU trade.

[55] In the same year the APSM was abolished. In the previous year the *Ministero delle Partecipazioni Statali* (Ministry of State Economic Participations) and the *Ministero per il Mezzogiorno* (Ministry for the *Mezzogiorno*) had both been abolished.

[56] In 1993 money stock grew by 7.9% (Banca d'Italia, 1995, *Considerazioni Finali*, p. 15). From November 1993 both ordinary and extraordinary Lombard loans on the current account at the Treasury were abolished by an Act of Parliament followiong the Maastricht Agreement.

[57] The devaluation of the lira was a consequence of the decision to introduce a restrictive monetary policy by the German monetary authorities. Given the perfect mobility of capital, numerous investors sold lire to purchase other currencies. Surprisingly the abrupt depreciation of the real exchange rate was not followed by a surge in inflation. But we can not forget the crucial role of speculation.

unemployment,[58] the previously announced fiscal policies and fears of a financial crisis all contributed to the contraction of demand. The impact of restrictive monetary policies was considerable, and was accentuated by tension in foreign exchange markets. In order to offer operators a precise quantity indicator from November 1992 to March 1993 the customary instruments of monetary control were combined with a system limiting and supervising the expansion of credit (Banca d'Italia, 1993, *Considerazioni Finali*, p. 14).

Interest rate growth, credit restrictions and monetary policies to dampen inflation, all of them exacerbated the cyclical downswing. The positive inflationary trend from December 1992 to December 1993, when prices rose by a mere 4.3%, was accompanied by an unfavourable cyclical trend. The inflationary impulse was limited not only by the weakness of internal demand but also by the consequences of the July 1992 settlement on the cost of labour, which provided for, among other things, the abolition of the sliding scale. Efforts by households to increase saving produced to a further fall in demand, which was already stretched by fears of a financial crisis: this magnified the decline in income.[59]

The slowdown in inflation and the marked improvement in the balance of payments strengthened the resolve of monetary authorities to progressively reduce the cost of money, in the desire to facilitate enterprises and foster employment. The discount rate started to descend in the final months of 1992.

The September 1992 devaluation curiously did not produce any visible effects on inflation in Italy. Indeed the currency depreciation fuelled inflation, both through the direct effect on the cost of imports and in so far as it allowed internal producers to increase profits, sheltered from foreign competition. However in 1993 these pressures were more than counterbalanced by the recession which squeezed profit margins and above all by the powerful deflationary impact of restraint on CLUP imposed by incomes policies[60] and the shrinking level of consumption.

---

[58] The persistent North-South divide fuelled the considerable distortions in employment, since the number of unemployed was higher in the southern regions, and thus it became vital to gain access to adequate information on the number of vacancies in the country as a whole.

[59] In 1993 household consumption decreased by 3% in real terms, disposable income fell by 5% and fixed investment fell by 11% (Banca d'Italia, 1995, *Considerazioni Finali*, p. 12).

[60] For a presentation of the evolution of incomes policy in Italy, as well as other interesting experiences, see Acocella (1995, chpt. 15).

The considerable impact of policy measures, somewhat surprising since they were both numerous and poorly constructed, fuelled negative expectations at a time when the European outlook was all but encouraging. Indeed the EU abruptly entered a recession from 1992 to 1993. This was followed by a tangible recovery and a greater surge in production than previously thought possible.

In 1993[61] the lira depreciated by 7%, favouring exports which had already risen sharply in the second half of 1992.[62] Nevertheless such strong export growth was insufficient to prevent a slump in internal demand and to boost production up from the level recorded at the end of the previous year.

In 1993 significant progress was made in readjusting public finance: the total borrowing requirement of the state sector fell from 10.6% to 9.8% of GDP net of interest payments. The state deficit rose from 0.6% to 1.8% of GDP (Banca d'Italia, 1994, *Considerazioni Finali*, p. 16).

3.3 Towards the new century

In 1994 the current account deficit, the additional debts of the state sector in foreign markets and purchases of bonds by non-residents were easily surpassed by the demand for foreign currency arising from outward capital flows.[63] The weak exchange rate boosted exports, although demand also grew as internal investments in plant and machinery and purchases of consumer durables rose. Growth in overall household consumption on the other hand was limited. The consequent expansion of value added was accompanied by a slight increase in productivity and a drop in employment. Significant changes were observed on the social front: whilst in the 1970s the flexible employment of labour was bitterly opposed by

---

[61] In the two year period between 1993 and 1994, households contributed on a massive scale to outward capital flows, partly through unit trusts. Firms accounted for net outflows of at least 600,000 billion lire, either directly or through the banking system in the form of foreign currency loans, and by investing a portion of export revenue abroad (Banca d'Italia, 1995, *Considerazioni Finali*, p. 13).

[62] In 1993 the currency fluctuation bands within the EMS, which Italy had left the previous year, were widened to ± 15%.

[63] Outward capital flows were mainly the result of uncertainty over the re-ordering of public finance. As reported by the media capital outflows, for which businessmen and hoteliers were principally responsible, were chiefly directed towards Austria and Germany, and huge sums of foreign currency were confiscated (but still the top of the iceberg).

trade unions, now greater flexibility coupled with more efficient use of plant was viewed as the appropriate mechanism for raising productivity. Nevertheless

> The revolt against bureaucratic routine and the search for flexibility created new structures of power and control, rather than creating the conditions for our freedom. (Sennet, 2000, p. 46)

The share of profits in industry recovered to 1988-89 levels, the highest since the early 1970s, while the service sector touched a record peak (Banca d'Italia, 1995, *Considerazioni Finali*, p. 17). The discount rate was finally raised to 9% in May 1994 after a number of changes. Retail prices, which were rising at a rate of 3.7% half way through the year (the lowest for the previous 25 years) had reached 4.1% by December 1994.

The first signs of the readjustment of public finance, despite rapidly rising public debt, represented the light at the end of the tunnel. In 1997 some 337,203 billion lire of new debt was issued, bringing the total to around 124% of GDP.[64] The consequences of such a distortion could only hinder the national economy. Indeed inflation began to gather pace once again, reaching 5.8% in 1995, as a result both of an increase in costs, in the form of imported inflation, and in demand generated by export growth.

In such complex circumstances, both the Bank of Italy and entrepreneurs became the target of what was at times extremely harsh criticism. On the one hand the bank was accused of not raising the discount rate to dampen the inflationary impulse caused by the deflation of the lira.[65] It was argued that exchange rate credibility would ease lira interest rates, with immediate benefits for the entire economy. On the other hand it was suggested that blame lay not with the Bank of Italy but rather with entrepreneurs, who unethically rigged profits. The surge in prices stemmed from demand pressure, which effectively signalled the end of the 1992 slump, to the extent that entrepreneurs could direct supply abroad, where higher profits were to be made from sales thanks to the exchange rate, or alternatively they could sell in the internal market at higher prices.

---

[64] The causes of this growth were the issue discount on government bonds, the repayment of previously issued debt and the depreciation of the lira in foreign exchange accounts.

[65] In the early months of 1995 strong speculation against the lira created a speculative bubble to all intents and purposes. At the end of March a reduction in the discount rate in Germany favoured a slight recovery of the lira. In Germany the volume of money declined in the early months of 1995. The increase in May of the same year was limited.

This provoked general criticism of the Italian entrepreneurial system, which was apparently preoccupied with short-term strategies rather than with long-term investment projects.

This crisis was essentially political and institutional, the most pressing issue being that of public debt and specifically its control, rather than its magnitude but rather in terms of its control. This was a fundamental difference with respect to Belgium:[66] no uncertainly existed in Belgian capital markets over the Government's ability to control the expansion of public debt.

Despite its autonomy the Bank of Italy was not in a position to guarantee that future governments would not resort to a monetary solution to resolve the central issue of public debt. Since yields on Italian debt in foreign currency were comparable with yields in other nations, financial markets subscribed to the view that the widespread holdings of public debt which were evenly distributed across the social classes, would not suffice to impede future coalitions from resorting to extraordinary financing. Hence the state of public finance became an inevitable reference point for the economy. Stabilisation of the debt seemed imminent, but international opinion remained sceptical about a renewed vicious circle. A positive signal came from the agreement on pensions[67] which revealed precisely how arduous it was for government authorities to curb public expenditure decisively. The credibility effect became so crucial that it heavily conditioned the exchange rate.

In 1994 it emerged rather curiously that private Italian firms in the private sector were investing more than their European counterparts.[68] However this increase was not sufficient to absorb growth in demand. On the other hand it probable that a substantial fall in the exchange rate would have led to a peculiar state of excess output capacity and would have revealed firms low net profitability of firms.

Within a more coherent analytical framework, we should not underestimate the effects of a one-off indirect tax levy and the increased

---

[66] Belgium, whose public debt was higher than Italy's in terms of GDP, had an exchange rate which was firmly anchored to the EMS parity and interest rates were only slightly higher than Germany.

[67] Payment of retirement pensions to 50 year olds appeared an unjustified and unproductive decision: no goods and services for the common good were obtained in exchange and they were offered to everyone in this age was eligible. Perplexity over the possibility of significantly reducing employee's expenses was comprehensible.

[68] Investments advanced by 6.8% in Italy compared to 4% in France and the United Kingdom; in Germany they decreased by 2.8%.

prices of imported inputs. Italian industry was specialised in the production of final rather than primary goods, importing principally from Germany and paying for such imports in overvalued marks. The repercussions on Italian foreign exchange reserves were appreciable and the term «easy profits» is perhaps rather hasty and not entirely appropriate. The profit trend was the result of the exchange rate and certainly not of internal demand, although the importance of the cost of capital must not be overlooked. Compared to the 1980s the cost of capital surged, the combined result of three factors: (a) the increase in real interest rates, (b) the increase in invested capital considered in relation either to added value or the number of wage-earners (neither can the theory of constant distribution with constant returns to scale be invoked here), and finally (c) the acceleration in the economic depreciation of capital goods.

In 1995, despite the fact that the surge in inflation was expected, it was nevertheless alarming. The increase was caused by the currency devaluation, as we have already seen, and magnified by the substantial rise in the price of raw materials[69] and imports, however it also boosted internal and external demand. Such a peculiar process in which output prices grew more than retail prices could have affected any country which devaluated its currency. But what was interesting here was that the phenomenon also affected countries which re-valued their currency; an indication of a general anomaly in industrial prices.

In Italy wages remained in line with incomes policies governing contractual variables, without precluding adjustments for market disturbances. Wages grew at a rate which was higher than forecasted inflation but a rate close to the rate of real inflation. Firms earned higher profits and thus undertook new investments. Productive capacity expanded as did the level of employment (in April 1995 300,000 new jobs were created). Increases in public tariffs and indirect taxation were imposed not to increase revenues and hence to reduce the deficit, but rather as a result of the need to cover the higher level of expenditure resulting from the devaluation.[70]

In such a complex state of affairs, the political uncertainty pervading the country played a decisive role and seriously undermined the credibility of policy makers, who were deemed to be incapable of adopting adequate

---

[69] The increase in the price of raw materials triggered a rise in the price of intermediate goods, which partially fed through to output prices (which increased by 8.2%) and retail prices which reached a level of 5.8% in June.

[70] The price of raw materials rose and the cost of servicing debt surged in the aftermath of the interest rate rises.

measures to restrain public expenditure: political stability thus became a prerequisite for economic stability.

At the end of July 1995 the Cabinet[71] approved a sweeping set of measures[72] later passed by Parliament to abolish 122 government licences, leaving only 9 in force.[73] On 3 August 1995 the Senate approved measures designed to accelerate the completion of public works and promote new projects in depressed areas (Decree Law 244/95).[74] The new norms focused on the importance of controlling planning and investment by local authorities, while the CIPE was empowered the power to revoke state funding to inefficient local government and allocate the funds elsewhere. Intervention in backward areas, also including areas in the centre and north, was assured by a series of incentives in the form of tax credits which could be obtained automatically by compensating tax debts under the new system. The maximum amount available was 60% of the highest level of aid granted by the EU.

In order to improve the financial structure of the *Piccola e Media Industria* (PMI, Small and Medium Sized Enterprises) in southern regions, a fund[75] was established to grant interest subsidies for the funding of short-term bank debt at 30 September 1994 and to guarantee such operations as well as to provide participation loans or the purchase of shareholdings. The revolving credit for PMI could be used for interest payments and to fund short-term debt of less than 5 years, up to a maximum of 3 billion lire.

---

[71] At the start of 1995 the rate of unemployment stood at 12.2% and in April of the same year at 12%. The recovery occured in the northern regions, and so recourse to CIG declined.

[72] As far as tax credits were concerned, the most important innovations were for industrial groups which were permitted to compensate debts and credits between different companies. Small firms and individuals could transfer credits to banks in exchange for loans or to another taxpayer who could then compensate the credit with amounts owed to the tax authorities. This option should make the long delays (the current average is approximately 6 years) in receiving rebates from the tax authorities a thing of the past. Over 900,000 individuals were exempted from filing annual income tax returns; tax relief on principal dwellings was extended, and measures were introduced limiting the need to issue delivery notes, receipts or invoices.

[73] These concerned gun licences, casinos, intellectual property, patents, driving and nautical licences, radio broadcasting, mobile telephones, VAT numbers, company ledgers and registers.

[74] This programme included the recently launched project for the container port of *Gioia Tauro* in Calabria (that is a region in the South of Italy), the subject of fierce political and economic battles.

[75] The funds were to be managed by a bank nominated by the Treasury.

Various amounts were also available over a number of years to build infrastructures. In addition to projects which co-financed with the EU, and in order to co-ordinate aid to individuals as well as firms and other collective bodies, territorial pacts were instituted by law to promote local development in depressed areas in accordance with the objectives approved by the EU Commission.

Government efforts and the sincerity of these intentions fostered substantial recovery of the lira against the mark on August 11 1995, eased by the strengthening of the dollar. This reassured foreign investors, and the return of the lira returning to the EMS no longer appeared so remote.

However inflationary pressure resurfaced in the second half of November 1995 when in nine sample cities an inflation rate of 6% was recorded in nine sample cities, the result of increases in the price of petrol, cars, tyres and furniture. Great concern arose both over the loss of competitiveness and for the difficulty in complying with Maastricht targets. The Italian situation now seemed more precarious as economic and monetary union loomed, and comprehensible fears of an inflation-devaluation-inflation spiral emerged. In 1995 the average rate of inflation in Italy was 5.4%.

At the end of 1995 the programme of public finance[76] for the following year was approved, with 3,800 billion lire of increased revenue and spending cuts of 1,485 billion lire, for a total of 5,285 billion lire, constituting a part of the 32,500 billion lire savings outlined in the government's 1996 budget.

In January 1996[77] it emerged that firms had earned considerable profits

[76] The series of measures were defined the "mini-manoeuvre" on account of their limited entity. The price of the scratch card lottery ticket increased from 2,000 to 2,500 lire, and the jackpot also increased. Stamp duty on the registration of deeds, land and mortgages increased from 150,000 to 250,000 lire. In terms of spending cuts, there was a reduction of 0.6% in tax credits on social security payments; the prices of pharmaceutical products with the identical properties were equalised; the travelling expenses of civil servants were reduced by 20%; the cash flow of *Ferrovie dello Stato* (State Railways) was redefined; the cash outlays of ANAS (the Highways Agency) were reduced; a 5% reduction was imposed on cash outlays for goods and services of ministries; spending on supply teachers in schools was also reduced. Other reductions in spending for a total of 2,350 billion lire were also planned.

[77] On 5 January 1996 Alberto Zuliani, Chairman of ISTAT, illustrated the new features of the system for gathering data on retail prices in the future. Various products were to be replaced or removed from the basket of goods, with new methods of collecting data and a new weighting pattern (the relative weight of foodstuffs fell from 22.26% to 21.95%). New distribution channels were also

during the previous year, partly due to the price rises.[78] This announcement provoked immediate reactions from trade unions. Again in January 1996 the retail price index based on a revamped basket of goods revealed retail price inflation of 5.5%, a decline in inflation with respect to the final months of the previous year. The fact that the devaluation of the lira did not have a negative impact on prices was somewhat surprising; but it is likely that the new statistical method of calculation influenced these results. Even if statistics are not what we would wish them to be, we be at a loss without them (Morganstern, 1963, p. 35).

On 26 March the *Decretone Previdenziale* (maxi-decree on social security) provided for government bonds (treasury bills) to be issued to pensioners in payments of arrears. Pensioners were entitled to sell the bonds to cash in the sums owed immediately.

At the end of May 1996 the lira remained strong in relation to the other major currencies (with the exception of sterling). Market optimism over the future of the lira continued and indeed the preference for the lira caused concern over possible speculation. The director general of *Confindustria*, Cipolletta observed that the return of the lira to the EMS would not so much avert the risk of devaluation as foster its revaluation. This however was not desired at the time, since the cyclical downswing called for lower interest rates: an excessively high exchange rate would have slowed growth.

On 20 June 1996 the measures approved by the Prodi government were introduced. On the revenue side[79] the principal changes were the introduction of a single tax rate of 27% on interest from bank deposits and deposit certificates[80] coupled with measures to prevent tax avoidance and restrictions on certain forms of tax relief.

included as observation points for recording retail price data. In 1992 changes had already been made to ensure that statistics on inflation were more realistic. Nevertheless this time with the introduction of new calculation methods the changes were more radical. ISTAT plans to evolve towards only one central price index in future, with subsidiary indicators for social categories, geographical areas and groups of products.

[78] Thus the phenomenon of profit-push inflation emerged, within the general category of cost-push inflation.

[79] The conflicting news concerning STET led the share price to plummet in August 1996. This was substantially an over-reaction to uncertainty.

[80] The lower tax rates on interest income from bonds and debentures of 12.5% made these assets more appealing. Serious concern over the credit market existed and the measures came at a time when growth in bank deposits was

In July 1996[81] an event that had not been witnessed for 28 years occurred: prices fell, at least according to statistics although faith in the latter was not absolute! Despite repeated revision and reshuffling the retail price index still manifested irresolvable contradictions.[82]

At the end of 1996 the German central bank significantly reduced the cost of money.[83]

The slowdown in the expansion of the German money supply and the absence of inflationary pressure enabled the *Bundesbank*[84] in a position to lower the spot against forward rate from 3.3% to 3%. This opening in short-term interest rates in Frankfurt was immediately exploited, not only by countries belonging to the mark area (Belgium, Holland, and Austria - not Switzerland) but also by France, with reduced pressure on bank lending which breathed new life into the feeble economy.

In August 1996 the price of oil rose and again in September the effect of events in Iraq produced a further 6% rise in the price of this strategic raw material. Concurrently president Clinton's decision to take military action in Arab territories caused the dollar to rise. The price of oil peaked at the beginning of September to $21.50 a barrel.

In Italy at the end of September 1996 the 1997 Financial Act was approved and was immediately dubbed the *Maxistangata* as it represented

---

sluggish. Tax leverage led to a process of disintermediation which undermined the central role of banks as credit intermediaries.

[81] In July 1996 firms, households, commercial credit companies and unit trusts took 10,000 billion lire out of the country, compared to the average of 3,500 billion lire "expatriated" each month. With the liberalisation of capital flows significant monthly fluctuations were recorded in monetary inflows and outflows, however this peculiar phenomenon may have been linked to the business cycle. Indeed the increase in the tax rates on interest income from deposit certificates to 27% may have induced many companies to abandon this type of investment in favour of investment overseas. The performance of the lira may also have induced firms and speculators to acquire foreign currency for use in future investments.

[82] For example the weight of rent income was lower than in reality life since it did not consider the implicit cost of owner-occupied dwellings; figures did not take discount policies into account and were based on official price lists; and it was difficult to make allowances for improvements in the quality of products. As a result, proof of inflationary dynamics could not be exhaustive.

[83] On 26 August 1996 the price of oil was raised to $18.85 a barrel. The rise was justified on the grounds of increased demand and repercussions on price dynamics were expected particularly in oil importing countries.

[84] For an analysis of the price trend in Germany see among others Pizzini and Nardi Spiller (2003).

a harsh blow for tax payers.[85] It provoked bitter debate in Parliament, and after its final approval on 22 December 1996 went down in history as the "European Financial Act" (with a total of 62,000 billion lire in savings) in memory of the «euro tax» which was levied in the name of future monetary union.

The situation in Italy was far from reassuring. Rising unemployment and the slowdown in inflation were accompanied by a reduction in wages. This was a well-known theoretical relation, the «death of inflation» (Bootle, 1996), which however in our opinion, offered concrete hopes of its revival.[86] In fact in September 1996 retail prices grew by 3.4% on a year on year basis.

In the second quarter of 1996 GDP declined by 0.4% with respect to the previous quarter. This was its lowest level since 1995, both in terms of the trend and the trade cycle; and Italy appeared to be entering a phase of stagnation. Figures for inflation in October 1996 in the sample cities revealed an annual growth rate of 3%, a decline compared to the previous 3.4% with a cyclical rise of 0.1% compared to the 0.3% of September. In August the foreign currency trade balance recorded a surplus of 7,580 billion lire; an increase from 6,170 billion lire in July. In October of the same year the Bank of Italy "cut" the discount rate which reached the level of 7.5%.

On 25 November 1996 Italy returned to the EMS, which it had abandoned in 1992, with a central parity of 990 lire to the mark. Firms felt penalised by what they considered the high exchange rate, although the effect upon imports was theoretically positive. We must stress that the Italian authorities initially tried to obtain a 1% higher exchange rate, and they succeeded in negotiating a considerably more favourable rate than was originally proposed. French opposition in particular was strong; and

---

[85] The Financial Act provided savings for a total of 37,500 billion lire of which 25,000 from public spending cuts and 12,500 billion lire in increased revenues, plus 13,000 billion lire levied with the so-called euro tax and a further 12 billion lire scraped from Treasury intervention. The overall saving amounted to 62,500 billion lire (the previous target was 32,500 billion lire). Added to the 15,000 billion lire savings with the manoeuvre in the summer needed to sort out the 1995 budget, the total amounted to 78,000 billion lire. This was an unprecedented effort imposed by the need to join the single currency. The Governor of the Bank of Italy Fazio committed himself to not raising interest rates until inflation was below the 3% threshold.

[86] See Nardi Spiller (1990a; 1990b; 1994; 1997) and Thurow (1996) among others. The latter author currently considers inflation to be an «extinct volcano», whilst we, if anything we would define it «dormant».

France insisted that the lira would drive out French exports with damaging effects on output.[87]

Exchange rate stability should have led to lower interest rates, which would have benefited enterprises by lowering interest expenses. However Italy's entry into EMU was not yet certain: the main issues at risk were the consolidation of public finance and restraint of inflationary pressure deriving from labour costs.[88]

At a Community level the Dublin Summit of 13 December 1996 focused on budgetary control in member states, underlining the need for strict control of public accounts. In the presence of deficits in excess of 2% of GDP, no sanctions were applicable if the economy in question was in a state of recession. If the decline in GDP was between 0.75% and 2%, sanctions were not applicable provided that concrete justification could be offered. Whereas if the decline in GDP was less than 0.75%, sanctions were to be applied automatically. Two types of sanction were established: preventive (to warn states going off course) and deterrent (the application of fines).

In December 1996 inflation settled at a trend of 2.6%, the same level as November. 1996 closed with an annual average rate of 3.9%, in line with Government targets. On 30 December the Cabinet approved additional budgetary measures amounting to 4,305 billion lire.[89]

In March 1997 further budget measures (15,500 billion lire of which 11,300 in spending cuts and 4,200 billion lire in extra revenue) were introduced. Subsequently this the Prime Minister announced the start of

---

[87] Effectively it was often said that a devaluation of the lira would damage the other economies. The French attack appeared to be unjustified. The generalised, and not just Italian, export boom was fuelled by massive demand for consumer and investment goods in South-East Asia. The financial incentives on the purchase of automobiles in France (in 1995 one and a half million lire were offered for the purchase of each new car) boosted Italian exports in view of the price and quality of our cars.

[88] On 25 November the news that the Prime Minister Mr Prodi was to be committed to trial shook the stock exchange. Financial and exchange markets recovery slightly the same day, and later stability was completely restored.

[89] These measures consisted of incentives on the purchase of new cars following the French model, 6% tax breaks on social security contributions in the South, continuation of benefits to road haulage companies for the whole of 1997, an increase in VAT on pharmaceuticals dispensed by the national health service, an increase from 20% to 25% of lump sum tax deductions and the abolition of the 100 million lire upper limit, incentives for the construction industry and livestock farming and an extension of the deadline for compliance with new norms on safety in the workplace.

discussions with social partners over the reform of the welfare state and the pension system. By June of that year an increase in raw material prices and labour cost per unit produced were predicted as a result of the rise in the dollar, with a possible peak in inflation which was however expected to settle at a rate of 2.3-2.4%.

At the end of September 1997 the 1997 Financial Act was passed and was immediately termed the «VAT Financial Act», since VAT rates were substantially altered. There were fears that these VAT increases (affecting petrol, telephone calls and wine) would have an impact on inflation, although as the Prime Minister Prodi explained the impact was in fact negligible, although he acknowledged the existence of tax-push inflation.

In the first half of 1997 the output trend was encouraging: overseas demand grew, internal consumption rose and turnover was positive (investments in equipment and capital increased, output of personal and consumer goods expanded). Nevertheless it was observed by *Confindustria* in particular, that for effective recovery these positive trends would have to continue throughout the year.

The fulfilment of public finance targets imposed by the Maastricht Agreement depended not only on the efficacy of corrective measures, but also on the ability to restrain the cost of public debt, in order to exploit the longstanding surplus in the primary balance.[90] At the end of March the fiscal policy manoeuvre was presented (16,000 billion lire, of which 11,000 billion lire in spending cuts and 5,000 billion lire in extra revenues) for approval by Easter. At the beginning of April the rate of inflation fell, but unemployment emerged concurrently as a growing problem, with the appearance of the «employee syndrome».[91] In May 1997 external accounts became positive once more following 20,354 billion lire of capital inflows, of which 20,184 were directed towards portfolio investments attracted by the high denomination of Italian bonds, the profitable yield compared to foreign equivalents, expectations of a drop in interest rates and renewed exchange rate stability.

The increase in purchasing power, upon which wages and salaries hinged,[92] had a negative impact upon the cost of labour, the effects of which were twofold. Firstly it jeopardised the arduous task of achieving a

[90] At a certain point public it was necessary for public debt to start growing at a rate lower than the rate of interest, to allow the public sector to record passive primary deficits, i.e. primary surpluses.

[91] For employment issues in European countries, see Modigliani, Moro and Sylos Labini (1998). Blanchard (1999) among others.

[92] In May 1997 the index of employees' hourly wages was 106.2 (December 1995 = 100) with an increase of 0.2% on April and 4.7% year on year.

further fall in the rate of inflation, and secondly it was not sufficient to reinvigorate stagnating internal demand and hence consumption. Contractual wages did not include extraordinary items (such as bonuses, overtime, company agreements, arrears or one-off payments).

On 28 June 1997[93] after a heated dispute the Governor of the Bank of Italy reduced the discount rate by 0.5%. However in the same month the tangible problems in Italy's productive apparatus resurfaced, with a decline in GDP and an inflation rate of just 1.4%.[94] Four explanations were offered for this: the diminished level of wage indexation resulting from the labour agreement, the independence of the Bank of Italy in its rigorous control of credit, the lower portion of public debt denominated in foreign currency and finally the greater awareness of the ruling political class. The decline in the inflation rate potentially paved the way for a virtuous circle, which would gently boost recovery of output and consumption, particularly since certain sectors of distribution, such as foodstuffs, were contributing decisively to the fall in prices.

In mid July 1997 data on the trade cycle was still negative despite a slight improvement in the second half with respect to the first half. There was a degree of recovery in ceramics and the mechanical industry, although even in these areas some firms were capable of adapting to the fixed exchange rate whilst others clearly lacked the strategic ability to adjust.

Once again in mid July the interest rate trend in Italy became conducive to a recovery in economic activity. Net yields on 6 or 12 month treasury bills were around 5.5%, with yields of 6.15%-6.21% on 3 or 5 year treasury bonds. By now there was only a 1% differential with respect to German bonds. Overseas debt presented no significant risks given the climate of optimism surrounding the entry of the lira into the single currency. Even if the inflation rate of 1.4% was likely to rise to 2% in the following months it was substantially under control. Real wages increased by 4.7% with respect to June of the previous year and thus were rising faster than non-adjusted output. The European lira exchange rate restrained the cost of imports. Unfortunately the high value of the dollar did nothing to lower the cost of raw materials from the dollar area. The first signs of strain were seen in profit margins and were the consequence of the unfavourable internal situation. The international economic outlook was

[93] On 22 June "surprisingly" the *Gazzetta Ufficiale* (Official Gazette) suppressed from the Italian currency the 1 lira coin which had not circulated for a considerable time.

[94] With reference once again to estimates by Balducci, Candela and Scorcu (2001, p. 409) during the decade 1988-1997 the sacrifice ratio was 13.5%.

positive, with recovery in Europe and a boom in America, while in international markets Italian output was being squeezed by the strong lira. Profits benefited from a reduction in the average lending rate.

Certain distortions in the Italian economy were difficult to correct. There were considerable delays in the process of privatization, resistance to the reform of the pension system and to the introduction of flexibility into the labour market.[95] The fiscal burden was also substantial. The flow of funds towards productive investments was limited and the level of public investment was low. Consumption by the middle classes, who bore the brunt of the high level of taxation, stagnated. The lower-middle classes were less vulnerable since same way thanks to the fact that public and private wages had increased faster than the rate of inflation. Nevertheless the boom in car sales was sufficient to pull the economy; and imports rose, partly the result of the inventory effect. Sadly investment in new technology, particularly in the South, was inadequate and in this area continued to battle against its traditional problems persisted.

In mid August sustainable growth coupled with the obsence of inflation in US economy prompted the FED to confirm existing monetary policy, while in Germany considerable uncertainty surfaced. The success of the American economy was the result of simple recipes focused towards the market, greater flexibility, a decrease in the role of the state and economic rigour. The result was an increase in industrial capacity and the first reduction in the cost of employment for nearly 50 years. These recipes however were not easily transferred to Europe. On 8 October 1997 Mr Greenspan's announcement that the US economy was overheating, caused the stock market to fall; expectations of an increase in US interest rates reduced asset prices to fall.

The Italian government stumbled into a crisis on 9 October 1997, initially with negative effects on the stock market; however expectations of a solution to the crisis prevented further turbulence. International financial markets were perturbed by the financial situation in South-East Asia (23-24 October 1997), triggered by a number of factors. The return of Hong Kong to China was certainly cause for concern, although the real crisis

[95] In August 1997 the hourly pay of employees increased by 0.2% over the previous month and by 4.6% year on year. The average of for the previous 12 months was +4.4%. This pay increase was higher than the 1.5% inflation recorded in August. Industrial action was rising (6.5 million working hours lost in the first 7 months compared to 2.6 million in the same period the year before). The French plan to reduce the working week to 35 hours with the same pay provoked debate over the introduction of a similar plan in Italy.

started in August 1997[96]. Years of excessive growth financed with foreign debt (too often invested in projects with doubtful returns) ended abruptly with capital outflows, the collapse of the exchange rate and stock market crashes. Austerity policies deflated the prices of financial assets and real estate, and threw the banking system into turmoil. Since 1983 the Hong Kong dollar had been anchored to the US dollar, a necessary condition to maintain the confidence of international investors in financial assets, in view of the transition to Chinese rule. In the light of negative expectations and the loss of confidence by investors pressure on the Hong Kong dollar induced authorities to raise interest rates from 5.5% to 10% in the same year. The economies of South-East Asia were thus squeezed by high interest rates and low growth rates: their stock exchanges lost a quarter of their value in just two months.

The unrest proliferated, the result of globalisation of stock markets. Shares in Telecom, the Italian telephone company initially peaked only to fall (losing 753 lire). Not even the dollar was spared (1693.02 lire) while the mark gained slightly (982.63 lire). Nevertheless New York did not panic since this phenomenon was considered to be a market, rather than a real, factor. Capital flowed out of South-East Asia and into US treasury bills, and it was hoped that a part would reach Italy in view of the strong economy (which was being pulled by the North) although household consumption was slack. The crisis in South-East Asia coupled with the demise of the Japanese giant Yamaichi was not considered sufficient to trigger a recession in the rest of the world, although the slow-down which affected a significant proportion of the world economy certainly left its mark.[97]

In Italy 1997 closed with an average inflation rate of 1.8% and a discount rate of 5.5% following a 0.75% reduction just before Christmas (23 December), the lowest level since 1973. Whilst inflation was in line with Government targets,[98] the price of certain goods and services were

[96] Whilst the Mexican economy was recovering from the crisis, a number of Asian states (Thailand, South Korea and Indonesia) experienced a financial storm to all intents and purposes. Given the close ties between banks and firm (the former offered funds to firms with strong political affiliations rather than solid investment projects) investors lost confidence. The risk premium on Asian assets grew, pushing up interest rates and causing exchange rates to collapse.

[97] The international scene was also upset by Niño (Bimbo), a peculiar atmospheric phenomena which appears roughly every five years before Christmas. By destroying crops, the prices of agricultural commodities rise, with effects on prices in importing countries.

[98] There was a fall in employment in November 1997 of 0.1% over the previous month, and 2.25 year on year. In the first few months of 1997 there was a 3.4%

subject to wide variations.[99] In 1997 the household propensities to save and to consume changed significantly with respect to 1996. The propensity to consume rose to 85.6%, with an increase of 1.9% over 1996, 8 points higher than the previous decade, whilst the propensity to save decreased to 14.4%: the lowest level since 1980. In its annual report on finance and local authorities, the Audit Office (*Corte dei Conti*) underlined the dramatic growth in local taxes: in 1996 the fiscal burden of local taxation rose by 5.4% - one and a half points above inflation.[100] In January 1998 the cost of labour reached 5.7% with inflation of 1.7%[101] and public debt equivalent to 122% of GDP; on 21 April the discount rate was lowered by 0.5% to 5%.

2 May 1998 was a historic date for the EU as it embarked upon the path towards further development and a higher level of employment with the birth of the «Euro 11».[102] At the same time financial markets were suffering the effects of the dollar-mark trade-off and in the short term a recovery of the dollar was expected. The advent of EMU implied the foundation and operation of one of the largest world markets in government bonds, which was destined to grow further. Future bond issues were to be denominated in euros and differences between the tax regimes operating in the stock markets of member states were destined to

year on year fall. In November employment in the tertiary sector declined by 0.1% on October and 1.8% year on year.

[99] Such as for example, post office tariffs which grew by 17% and the cost of an overnight train accommodation rose 8% compared to 1996. The cost of electricity measure in KW/hour dropped on average by 3%, as did telephone services which as a result of competition between fixed phones, mobile phones and international companies cost users 1% less. The various goods contained in the basket were thus subject to quite different types of price change.

[100] The fact that in June 1998 the trend of inflation in the 11 Euro states was 1.4% was comforting, and the same as May. In the 15 countries of the EU the rate was 1.6%.

Until the end of 1994 the EC had only twelve member states. From 1 January 1995, Austria, Finland and Sweden joined. Currently the term European Union is more common.

[101] The price per barrel of crude oil fell to $12 (12 March 1998).

[102] The eleven countries were Italy, France, Belgium, The Netherlands, Luxembourg, Spain, Portugal, Ireland, Austria and Finland, joined by Greece on 1 January 2001. The United Kingdom, Denmark and Sweden chose to remain outside.

disappear. The new currency[103] which was soon to be used in trade represented a unique challenge to the traditional supremacy of the dollar.

Nevertheless substantial perils exist and should not be overlooked,[104] one of which was the issue of rounding up or down. Although in macroeconomic textbooks aggregation leads to compensation, an underlying problem remains which if sufficiently grave, may cause prices to rise. It is our opinion that in reality upward price movements are more significant and decisive than downward price movements, and a warped spirit of innovation may induce individuals to take advantage of the situation. The common introduction of the euro will enable comparisons between wages in the same sectors of different countries and may favour catching up in the most productive sectors, whereas in fact wages should vary quite independently in relation to their relative weight in national output structures. Consequently, in order to avoid inflation in the labour market, incomes policies co-ordinated at a national level which reflect European directives to minimise the negative impact of uncoordinated wage bargaining would be more appropriate than coercive methods. In view of these considerations, it is vital to keep inflation[105] under control otherwise a sudden surge may seriously undermine such efforts.

Despite the slowdown in inflation the Italian economy was unable to take off and lagged behind the 3% growth rate in other member states. The crisis in South-East Asia depressed international trade in general, however in Italy the heavy tax burden and rigidities in the labour market were mainly responsible. In turn manufacturing capacity was weak and interest rates were slow to fall. State incentives offered on the purchase of new cars supplemented consumption although the potential efficacy of incentives for building was limited in the light of the decline in the propensity to save.

---

[103] The experience of monetary union in Europe has certain precedents such as for example the «Latin League» in the second half of the 19th century, already treated in Nardi Spiller (1991a; 1991b; 2000b). For issues relating to the creation of a supra-national currency, see among others Cencini (1995, *parte* III).

[104] This aspect concerns the prices of products with a low unit cost or services such as unit costs for telephone calls, kW hours of electricity or cubic metres of gas or water. Furthermore price stability which undoubtedly restrains the price of goods imported from EMU states, initially at least, must withstand the huge costs of converting administrative and financial procedures and information systems.

[105] The change in the cyclical trend in May was principally the result of the application of contractual pay rises by oil companies, banks and private schools.

Black Friday hit the stock exchange on 21 August, sparing no-one, as an intrigue of political events subdued the markets.[106] South-East Asia had been engulfed in a violent crisis for more than a year and had reached a state of total uncertainty. The not entirely unexpected «Russian effect» heavily conditioned the European economies. Russia had debts totalling $30 thousand billion with Germany, and the spectre of a financial crisis spread as far as the Johannesburg stock exchange as well as to markets in South America. Concern over these events had a negative impact upon employment which had been showing signs of distortions at a European level for a long time.[107]

In such disturbing circumstances the German banks maintained a calm stance in the face of significant exposure. Experience of the financial crisis of the 1980s had prompted banks to grant only loans guaranteed by the federal government (95% of financial exposure was guaranteed by the *Landesbanken*). A degree of certainty was also afforded by the origins of the Russian crisis, since the economy had suffered the effects of external shocks. In the first half of 1998 the value of Russian exports, particularly of raw materials, fell 13% on a year on year basis, from $40.7 to $35.4 billion. The main cause was the fall in world prices in general, and raw

[106] These were a combination of political factors, such as terrorism, the American raids in the Arab territories, international tensions, media effects such as the Sexgate scandal, and natural disasters, first and foremost the flooding in China. The OPEC crude oil price continued to fall although in July production was curtailed. In mid August 1998 the OPEC countries announced a 61 cent reduction in the price per barrel to $11.60. Previously OPEC itself had indicated a reference price of $21 a barrel for the month of July.

[107] In order to make the labour market more flexible without unconditionally accepting the Anglo-Saxon model of complete deregulation Germany decided to experiment the «*Kombi-Lohn*» for a period of four years. This was a form of mixed salary, whereby those unemployed for more than a year and a half could accept employment at the minimum wage level (53 to 57 per cent of the previous wage) and would receive a further 20% paid for by the welfare state. In this way wages would amount to a respectable 73-77% of previous wages. This alternative was more attractive than the so-called McDonald's jobs, i.e. jobs at the lowest end of the wage scale which had allowed the USA to achieve an unemployment rate of 5% (less than half the European average), but with drastic cuts in income. On the other hand excessive deregulation of labour markets and fears of possible unfair wage competition stigmatised the phenomenon of social dumping. On the latter see Tsoukalis (1997, p. 326).

material prices in particular, of which Russia was a major exporter.[108] There were inevitable repercussions on the balance of payments and massive capital outflows. This led to the devaluation of the rouble, however the real problem was masked by the devaluation: there was a growing conviction that international financial institutions were powerless. The IMF did intervene, albeit rather clumsily, by asking Russia to set its public accounts in order, by increasing taxation and reducing expenditure as well as strengthening its commitment to curbing inflation by means of wage restraint. However an increase in the tax burden and a reduction in expenditure generated a grave internal liquidity crisis. Russian banks had lent large sums in cash and found themselves in financial difficulty: to avoid bankruptcy they attempted to sell their liquid assets, namely Russian treasury bills (GKO). The result was a slump in the value of the latter, which forced the Russian central bank to raise interest rates to 180%: the spectacular collapse of the rouble was inevitable.[109]

Italy was the only member of the euro area with a negative rate of GDP growth, yet it seemed to produce more wealth than official figures suggested: the black economy played an important role and if this activity were to be regularised it would make room for a decrease in the tax burden.

Unexpectedly on 26 October the Governor of the Bank of Italy, Mr Fazio lowered the discount rate by 1% (to 4%). Nevertheless growth in the Italian economy was limited: 1.5% against the 2.4% forecasted. Italy was suffering the effects of the international recession, particularly in terms of the decline in exports to South-East Asia and the simultaneous increase in imports. Internal demand contracted following the abolition of incentives on the purchase of cars and weak disposable income. Public debt was still at extremely high levels and thus it was extremely difficult to relax budgetary rigour in order to create new jobs. Consequently, in addition to structural policies, there was a clear need for effective policies to stimulate demand.

In November[110] the rate of inflation in Italy fell to 1.5% compared to 1.7% in October, coupled with a 2.1% drop in labour cost which was

---

[108] During the first part of 1998 the Russian price of oil fell on average by 33%, that of natural gas by 16%, iron ore by 11%, coal by 24%, nitrogenous fertilisers by 42%, timber by 24% and copper and nickel by 20%.

[109] As Soros (certainly not an outsider considering his speculative role in this event) underlined in his letter to the *Financial Times* of 13 August, at the time it was vital for the IMF to inject liquidity, which it failed to do.

[110] On 17 November 1998 the Federal Reserve decided, not unexpectedly, to lower interest rates: the discount rate fell down to 4.5%, and the FED rate to 4.75%.

attributed to the introduction of IRAP (a Regional Tax on Productive Activities).[111] On 3 December the discount rate was lowered to 3.5% in line with the level of 3% set by the EU.[112] Banks automatically reduced the prime rate, and mortgage rates and other interest rates followed suit. However this reduction in the cost of money did not boost output and sufficiently restore «animal spirits».

News of a drop in the price of crude oil to $10 a barrel raised spirits in December 1998 (a 26% reduction). However immediately after the start of British and American hostilities in Iraq, the price crept back up to $11 a barrel, although this was still relatively low. In the long-term low prices would have led to the closure of certain wells and a reduction in supply, so further price rises were expected at a later date.

Shortly before Christmas, Mr Fazio lowered the discount rate to 3%. The Governor's decision had been expected, to comply with EU rates[113] and at the end of 1998 the value of the euro was set at 1,937.26 lire.

While labour cost per employee totalled 118.4 million lire in 1997, 25% higher than in other European countries, in 1998 it declined to 114.2 million lire. A 6.6 million lire saving in health service contributions, now included in IRAP accounted for this fall.

In the euro area, economic activity declined in the second half, although consumption held up throughout the year. Investment slowed in the final quarter. Exports to the euro area, which expanded particularly rapidly in 1997 and also grew in 1998, declined at the end of the year. Imports followed a similar trend. It was the Italian and Germany economies that suffered most from the downswing in the trade cycle, with a fall in GDP in the final quarter. In Italy the inflation rate remained slightly below 2% for the whole of 1998. Despite continuous wage increases, CLUP in manufacturing industry rose as a result of the limited increase in

---

[111] This was introduced in the 1998 tax year, and was a direct tax replacing five other taxes or contributions (health service contributions, ILOR - Local Income Tax -, IPI - Company Property Tax -, ICIAP - Local Property Tax on Business Premises -, and the tax on VAT registration numbers) which individuals and legal entities were subject to pay. Its contribution to the reduction in labour cost and hence to an increase in employment was to be assured by the abolition of the national health service contributions paid by employers and by wage-earners. In reality this was not the case, as IRAP could not be deducted from income and thus generated an automatic increase in IRPEG.

[112] On 12 December 1998 the Governor of the Bank of Italy lowered the legal interest rate from 5% to 2.5%.

[113] There was considerable pressure on spot against forward rates and the yield on 6 month treasury bills fell to 2.85%, half the level of previous years.

productivity, while in other member states it fell. Nevertheless internal employment[114] increased with the introduction of greater flexibility in the labour market, which was gradually incorporated into legislation and collective labour agreements. There was particular growth in the number of new fixed term contracts, and it was observed that the transformation of the labour market is taking the form of a structural adjustment (Banca d'Italia, 1999, *Considerazioni finali*, p. 28).

In terms of international liquidity, derivatives made it possible to manage risk more effectively, and this led to an increase in the velocity of circulation of internal and foreign money, and growth in the level of world liquidity. By greatly expanding transactions in stock markets and foreign exchange markets, derivatives could however accentuate the inherent instability in the economy during periods of crisis. This meant that non-bank operators with high borrowing power in relation to their capital became of particularly important since changes in the composition of their portfolios could destabilise even the medium-sized economies (Banca d'Italia, 1999, *Considerazioni finali*, p. 11).

In 1998 both nominal and real interest rates fell on all world markets with the general improvement in public finance and the fall of inflationary expectations, but also as a result of a decline in the level of economic activity.

The Russian crisis in August led to speculative currency movements, initially outside the euro area and later affecting two euro countries, one of these being Italy.

At the end of 1998 and the start of 1999, although the South American crisis remained to be fully resolved,[115] signs of a recovery emerged in South-East Asia. A number of influential sources, including the President of Italy Mr. Ciampi, confirmed that there was no further fears of the «tequila effect» from Mexico and no connection with the previous crisis in Mexico.

The outlook in Italy was far from reassuring. On 15 January 1999 a number of price increases were announced.[116] Growth in the Italian

[114] In Italy there are many self-employed workers and a large number of small firms. For a general analysis of the prospects for growth in European employment, see Commissione delle Comunità Europee (1994).

[115] On 13 January 1999 the Brazilian stock market crashed. Continuous capital outflows from Brazil effectively devalued the real. In an attempt to support the currency, the Brazilian central bank intervened by selling dollars. However on January 15 the real was officially devalued, with a beneficial impact on the Brazilian stock exchange.

[116] Unleaded petrol increased by 32 lire a litre, leaded petrol by 10 lire, diesel oil increased by 40 lire and natural gas by 3 lire per m^3. These increases were

economy was limited, although this discouraging news was ameliorated by the fact that positive results that had been achieved in adjusting state balances. In 1998 the deficit/GDP ratio was an apparent standstill, at a rate of 2.68%, virtually the same level as 1997 coupled, with marginal GDP growth of 1.4% (compared to 1.5% in 1997). The ratio of debt to GDP continued to fall, and in 1998 debt represented 118.7% of GDP (compared to 122.4% the previous year). The Treasury cut interest rates on post office bonds to 3% gross.[117]

The crude oil price trend was reassuring, with a price of $8 a barrel on 1 March 1999, compared to $33 twenty years earlier. In order to boost the languishing economy, the ECB lowered interest rates on 8 April 1999 bringing the spot against forward rate to 2.5%.

Despite this in July 1999,[118] Italian inflation perked up again[119] as a result of higher rents, more expensive insurance policies and rising petrol prices; on an annual basis the inflation rate reached 1.7%, compared to a European average of 1.1%.

Industrial production grew sharply in August. The index increased by 10.7% on a year on year basis, and the daily index increased by 7.3% since

approved by the Cabinet following recommendations from the CIP. The new prices came into force at midnight, and were the consequence of the so-called carbon tax (on pollutant emissions). The Finance Minister, Mr Visco forecasted extra revenue in excess of 2,310 billion lire, of which 1,000 billion lire were to be used to cover labour cost (0.82%), 700 billion lire were to be used to cover tax breaks and 300 billion lire were to be allocated to the environment.

[117] Measures introduced on 1 March fixed the gross annual interest rate at 3% for ordinary personal savings books and ordinary bearer savings books, electronic portfolios and special savings books for Italians resident overseas. The gross annual interest rate on personal savings books and bearer savings books which could not be accessed for at least three years was fixed at 3.25%.

[118] On 21 May 1999 AIMA (the Public Corporation Responsible for Managing Agricultural Markets) was abolished.

[119] In mid March 1999 (16 March 1999) the basket of goods used to calculate the consumer price index for blue and white collar workers was radically modified. With a new reference base, ISTAT was also compelled to change the weighting system, i.e., the relative weight of each good in the overall calculation of the inflation rate. Camomile tea, dried figs, gentlemen's hats, petticoats, honey, clothes pegs, brandy, camping stoves, electric razors and baby food were removed from the basket, while fast-food meals, contact lenses, tortellini, dog shampoos, chiropodists, pedicures, ballet and swimming lessons, disco admission fees, electronic games, motorcycle insurance policies, air conditioners, frozen pizza, internet subscriptions, microwave oven and other products were included.

it took an extra day's production into account. However this data should not be considered excessively encouraging considering that the new organisation of the production cycle explained the higher number of working days (between 2 and 3) compared to the previous year. In addition a number of firms staggered holidays at different times of year.

On 8 September 1999 the EU Labour Commission declared Italy and Greece to be the most backward countries in terms of their employment policy, the leading countries being Sweden, Belgium, Great Britain, Denmark and Ireland. This compelled Italy was compelled to introduce appropriate policies to promote youth employment, to combat long-term unemployment and to reform employment offices. At the same time it also became essential to reduce payroll taxes, reassess the pension system and enforce equal rights. Italy's long-standing problem of the *Mezzogiorno* returned to the forefront yet again: with its deteriorating unemployment problem. In the first half of September, inflation loomed on the horizon once more, following increases in the price of gas and electricity. These increases were in theory due to be compensated by subsequent measures to reduce the cost of essential services by 17%, with effect from January 2000. The rising price of petrol, and other products, including water, triggered fears of a renewed inflationary spiral.

The bullish gold price[120] had a positive impact on stock markets and the share price of companies operating in the gold sector. The eleven central banks of the euro area, the ECB, and the central banks of Great Britain, Sweden and Switzerland opted not to sell gold for the following five years, with the exception of previously planned sales: 400 tons a year, for a total of 2 thousand tons in the five year period. Investors greeted the news with enthusiasm and purchases resumed.

At the end of September the increase in fuel prices was confirmed, with a visible impact on inflation.[121] The high price of petrol raised fears over the cost of living index, price dynamics and rekindled a trade union dispute: while Mr Larizza, leader of UIL, confirmed the need to reconsider controlled prices for the products which tend to inflate prices rise, Mr

[120] However during the summer gold fell to its lowest level for 20 years, after the Bank of England's decision to sell a significant portion of its reserves. On 28 September 1999 the London gold fixing price reached $301.50 per ounce. After trading in the US gold reached a price of $309. The previous day before in Europe gold had recorded its highest increase in one day of the last 15 years reaching $281.10.

[121] In September internal growth was a mere 0.1%, increasing on an annual basis from 1.75 to 1.8%. The decision by certain companies to differentiate between the price of diesel and the price of petrol was comforting.

D'Antoni, leader of CISL, strongly opposed such a move, underlining the need to bring fuel back under the control of the Energy Authority.

Mr Greenspan's declarations on 15 October 1999 concerning a possible return to inflation in the US, particularly in view of the forthcoming Christmas festivities[122] caused turbulence on stock markets, which were already strained by the crisis in Far East. Expectations of interest rates increases were justified, and on 18 October the principal European stock markets[123] fell by between 1% and 2%.[124]

At the end of October 1999 concerns over Italian inflation grew, alongside fears that Maastricht parameters could not be complied with. Inflation effectively increased in October: the retail price index calculated using data from sample towns revealed an increase of 1.9% over the previous year.[125]

On World Saving Day Mr Fazio[126] confirmed that the Italian rate of inflation was higher than the euro area average, and that this was partly due to the structural problems which prevented Italy from realising its full growth potential. This was reflected in the price trend. Structural reforms were clearly required to lower the tax burden.

The ECB implemented a credit squeeze on 4 November: the interest rate was increased from 2.5% to 3%, in relation to inflationary expectations and the general increase in the money stock.

Data from the Italian tax authorities was reassuring. Tax receipts in 1999 had taken even the Finance Ministry by surprise: receipts were 7,500

---

[122] The inflation rate in the US was fairly reassuring, with a higher growth rate was higher than in Europe. However there were signs of weakness in the US economy, so evidence of a slowdown was not to be underestimated.

[123] There was considerable demand for shares when ENEL was privatised (shares traded at a price of 60,000 lire).

[124] On 18 October 1999 Nissan, 35% controlled by Renault, announced a 30% cut in car output from 2002, with a 21% reduction in employment (21,000 job losses).

[125] Upward movements were caused by certain sectors: clothing and footwear, housing, water, energy and fuel, hotels, restaurants and public services. The main culprit however was oil. In addition to the increase in the price of petrol, insurance premiums also rose. On 22 October the news that the oil price was to rise suddenly by 3.3% to over $23 a barrel presented a serious threat to prices.

[126] In dealing with the merger between two large insurance groups, *Generali* and INA (National Institute of Assurance), Mr Fazio stated that the aggregation of large insurance companies could lead to changes in the holdings of certain banks, with further consolidation of leading banking groups.

billion lire higher than forecasted. This enabled the government to plan a number of tax reductions.[127]

In November inflation settled at 2%.[128] At the beginning of December 1999 the euro fell considerably against the dollar. This caused concern in the euro area, since the EU lacked an institution which was responsible for taking immediate and decisive action. On 16 December the Financial Act was passed by the Chamber of Deputies and the Senate.[129] Prices remained under control, although the long-standing and crucial issue of the North-South gap worsened. The two areas were developing at different rates, which only served to exacerbate the unemployment problem in the South.[130] In southern regions, unlike in the rest of the country, the limited move towards the introduction of greater flexibility in the labour market (fixed term and part-time contracts) had a negative impact on more traditional forms of employment. Investment in the South grew by 1.9% in 1999 (compared to 3.2% in the Centre-North), mainly as a result of incentives for building work. The fact that investment was less dynamic in the South led to a pronounced imbalance: in 1991 investment in the South constituted 28% of the national total, while in 1998-99 this figure fell to 22%.

In financial markets the price of government bonds started to fall as fears of imminent interest rate rises grew;[131] this however did not have a

[127] In fact in 2002 tax deductions for dependent children are due to increase, from the current figure of 336,000 lire to 552,000; payroll taxes should decrease by 0.8%. The carbon tax is expected to be limited, and the cost of reducing payroll taxes is due to be covered by other resources.

[128] The price of fuel however continued to rise.

[129] Consumer associations reported price rises with the new year, caused by the increases in third party liability motor insurance, heating oil and railway tariffs. An increase in airport taxes was also expected, and was dubbed the «Jubilee tax», although the fact that the tax was to be applied until 31 December 2000 was baffling.

[130] In the context of increasing employment, there was specific reference to the opportunities offered by tele-working, particularly in the Public Administration.

[131] At the time the increase in the price of oil sparked fears of renewed inflation, and there were expectations of imminent interest rate rises. At the end of December 1999 the price of both leaded and unleaded petrol rose slightly. The high petrol price had an impact on inflation, partly because it increased producer prices (although this may be explained in part by the increased demand for intermediate goods). Surprisingly wages grew less than inflation, so that for the six month period following November 1999, it was forecasted that in the absence of further contracts were renewed, the percentage change in the hourly wage index in the economy as a whole would be similar to the November level

negative effect on share prices. In accordance with expectations, the price of government bonds, and of fixed interest bonds in particular, fell significantly. The principal stock exchanges on the other hand climbed to record levels, owing to the great interest in high-tech, telephony and internet stocks, at a time when interest rate forecasts should have generated an entirely different trend. In the euro area, the M3 money supply expanded considerably (+6.2% in November, compared to +5.8% in October) so that a rise in interest rates was expected.[132] Subsequently the European stock markets fell sharply as a result of massive sales in the aftermath of the Wall Street crash on 4 January. There was pressure on almost all the leading securities and trading on the New Market was suspended on account of the excessive price falls.

From 1991 to 1998 GDP grew by a mere 8.5%, only slightly more than 1% on an annual basis.[133] This put Italy in third last place at a world level behind Switzerland and Japan[134] with growth rates of 4.3% and 7.2% respectively. Growth in Italy[135] was much lower than in the other EU member states, which recorded an average of 14%. However industrial production was more encouraging, with growth of 8.2% year on year in December 1999. Overall in 1999 industrial production grew by 0.1% with respect to the previous year. European output growth was also encouraging: Belgium, Germany, Spain, France, Ireland, Italy, Luxembourg, the Netherlands and Finland all recorded rates of growth in excess of government forecasts contained both in the Stability Pact and in previous estimates. This was particularly surprising when we consider that in certain member states, including Italy, economic growth was below forecasted levels.

(+1.9% compared to the 2% inflation trend). The price of oil fell on 7 January 2000, with beneficial expects, as would be expected, on the price of petrol.

[132] The need to consider the fact that inflation, in terms of the choice of monetary policy, inflation consists of average, generalised price growth, focuses scientific interest on CPIcore. The latter tends to equal the sum of: 0.6 x CLUP + 0.3xM3 + 0.1x demand. With the exclusion of volatile components, such as energy or foodstuffs, we exclude relative price variations most frequently affecting price growth, but not all prices, which are less relevant to the ECB when it is tuning its monetary policy. See Wynne (1999).

[133] The highest rate of growth was in Ireland, with GDP growth of 66.8% between 1991 and 1998, followed by Poland, with growth of 42.5%.

[134] In the US growth of 24.2% was recorded, and in Canada of 20%. The average for OECD countries was 18.3%.

[135] Italy was also lagging behind in terms of growth in consumption: 7.3%, putting Italy in third last place, again ahead of Switzerland. The highest level of growth was recorded in Ireland.

In such a rapidly evolving situation, it was vital to remove all obstacles to the competitiveness of the European economy, such as the excessive fragmentation of goods and capital markets, particularly the market for financial services. It was also essential to remove bureaucratic and administrative barriers hindering the foundation and development of new enterprises. Massive state subsidies in certain sectors which distorted competition also needed to be abolished. Italy gave the impression of being a non-competitive economy: foreign capital was deterred by the excessive rigidity of the labour market; given the situation in the Ukraine there were stock market fears of a «dominoes effect» (and of a possible Ukrainian default on bonds). Since stock markets were interrelated, issues such as these spread at great speed. The dreaded announcement of the Ukrainian default failed to materialise, and the Ukraine, with the support of Ingank (the Dutch bank responsible for the numerous bond issues) presented a recovery plan to the financial community in mid February. This consisted of swapping the high yield eurobonds reaching maturity in 2000 and 2001 with 7 year bonds (bearing a 10% or 11% nominal interest rate) with a quarterly coupon; interest was to be paid from the following year.

In January 2000 the inflation rate[136] in Italy rose to 2.2%, the highest level for three years. This rekindled fears of subsequent inflationary pressure.

In keeping with sensations in the stock markets, Mr Greenspan announced a 0.25% rise in the interest rate on 2 February 2000. This decision was immediately followed on February 3 by a similar announcement from the ECB, which raised the discount rate once again in March in the face of possible inflationary pressure.

In February 2000, inflation in Italy reached a level of 2.4%, once again as a result of the increase in the price of oil.[137] The euro fell against the dollar and the risk of inflation threatened the whole of Europe. This was particularly alarming in view of the need to comply with Maastricht parameters, and indeed the Italian government endeavoured to persuade social partners to accept wage settlements in line with forecasted inflation rather than real inflation. There was however significant growth in industrial production in Italy (+1.5% over January). Compared to February

---

[136] In January 2000 ISTAT overhauled the basket, as it does every year, to correspond more closely to the consumption habits of the Italians.

[137] The price of crude oil rose from the beginning of March, to $31 a barrel, and this in turn caused an increase in the price of petrol.

1999, industrial production[138] grew by 7.7%: not since 1995 had a similar increase been recorded.

The performance of the NASDAQ share index was also rather curious, as an abrupt fall on 15 March which dragged down European technology stocks.[139] As Mr Thurow explained in a talk show,[140] the high-tech sector was inherently unstable, a feature typical of advanced sectors. He compared it with a roller-coaster ride: investors should be ready «to go up one minute and come down the next», never relying on certainty.

14 April was yet another black Friday on Wall Street, and was destined to be remembered in American financial history as a symbol of the intrinsic dangers of speculative bubbles. Both the NASDAQ and Dow Jones indexes were overwhelmed by the financial crisis.[141]

The return to bearish financial markets was preceded by a fall in European markets: in Milan the stock exchange lost 2.3%, in Frankfurt 3.1% and in Paris 3.2%. However whilst the negative trend on European stock markets did not cause particular concern, Wall Street was taken by panic. Sales of technology stocks had a negative effect on companies such as Microsoft, while the collapse of more traditional shares damaged the financial sector in general and the banks in particular.

This dramatic situation may have been influenced by Mr Greenspan's announcement on 13 March expressing concern over the current speculative bubble and the excessive level of economic growth, when he declared himself to be in favour of a rise in interest rates. The following day the he went a step further and invited banks and other financial institutions to make financial provisions for shocks on stock markets, warning that if one the one hand technological innovation had contributed to the minimisation of risk, on the other it did not protect investors from sudden confidence crises. Investors themselves were undoubtedly jointly

---

[138] The most dynamics sector were wood, transport, and the production of metal, rubber and plastics.

[139] Here we should remember that the announcement of an agreement between FIAT and General Motors was not well received by investors, and the FIAT share price fell.

[140] The details of the interview were published by the *Corriere della Sera* newspaper on 16 March. See Thurow (2000).

[141] The technological share index fell 356 points, roughly 10%, in addition to the 770 points lost in previous sessions. This new level was considerably below the danger level. The industrial share index lost 617 points, equivalent to 5.64%, and dropped to 10,307. The NASDAQ index was down 34.25% on the record level of March 10, and the Dow Jones index lost 15%, the greatest fall of all time.

responsible for their abuse of safety margins and for not protecting themselves adequately. Mr Greenspan's aim was to bring the excessive level of US growth down with a "soft landing", and in pursuing this aim he strove to limit the increase in the cost of money to between 3.5% and 4% (US interest rates rose by 0.5%).

In Italy[142] by mid June the inflation rate had reached a level of 2.5% (the rise was to be attributed to the cost of heating, fuel and transport), compared to an EU average of 1.9%. At the end of June inflation reached an annual rate of 2.7%, the consequence of rising fuel, cinema and restaurant prices. In July 2000, there was a welcomed fall. Indeed from a level of 2.7% in June, the inflation rate declined to 2.6% and then touched 2.5% in August.

Nevertheless the strong dollar, the weakening euro and the higher price of crude oil rekindled fears of inflation. There was a rise in output and productivity in the United States, which boosted consumption, increased absorption and suggested towards possible growth in demand in the countries which supplied the US. Fears of inflation were therefore well-founded, particularly in view of the fact that oil prices and public tariffs were rising.

In the third week of September, the euro plummeted below 0.8477 to the dollar and pushed the dollar up to 2,294 lire, while oil prices soared to record levels ($37 a barrel). Petrol prices in Italy began to creep up once more.

The IMF warned that the high price of crude oil presented a major threat to the international economy, and urged the ECB to intervene in support of the single currency; and in doing so it irritated Germany. Italy was poised to make emergency plans. On 1 September the ECB increased interest rates by .025% to 4.5%, in the hope of cushioning the fall of the euro and dampening the inflationary impulses caused by the price of oil and the depreciation of the European currency.

In this, the era of the new economy[143] and silicone, the oil price had lost none of its importance! Over the past decade global demand for crude oil had grown at an annual rate of 1.4%. During the three year period from 1995 to 1997, prior to the first crisis in South-East Asia, demand grew 2.5%. At the time two factors played a decisive role in maintaining global consumption: the rapid growth in South-East Asia (with demand rising at

[142] At this time the IRI closed down, after 67 years of activity. The death of Enrico Cuccia, the Chairman of *Mediobanca* who was considered the "guardian" of Italian capitalism, also represented a watershed in Italian finance.

[143] For an immediate introduction to the new economy see Rampini (2000) and Vaciago and Vaciago (2001).

an annual rate of 5%) and the solidity of the US economy. With growth in demand, oil became increasingly important in the world economy. Every $5 increase in the price of oil was equivalent to a 0.2% fall in economic growth over 2 years.

Inflation appeared to settle at a rate of 2.5% in September, lower than the rate of 2.6% recorded in July and August and 2.7% in June.

On 5 October 2000 the ECB raised interest rates by a quarter of a point once more. This measure raised doubts: monetary action would certainly not solve the rigidities in the system which were the underlying cause of inflation, and the rise in interest rates would limit growth and hence investment.

The year end was far from encouraging and the international economy was in recessive phase. At a global level the business cycle moved upwards in the first half of the year but this was dampened in the second half by the rising price of oil and the slowdown in the US economy. The European economy benefited from the marked devaluation of the euro, which favoured exports despite creating the risk of financial outflows. On the other hand trends in 2000 showed that for the ninth consecutive year growth in Italy was almost one percent below levels recorded on average in the other European states. The cause of this situation were the as yet unresolved structural problems. These included the excessive tax burden on enterprises undermining their international competitiveness (the profitability of Italian firms is the lowest in Europe); rigidity and excessive protectionism in the labour market which discouraged firms from taking on personnel and encouraged them to remain small; and the technology gap which has led to the shortage of workers to fill high-technology jobs in the Italian market. These three factors are crucial in explaining the substantial lack of profitable, high-tech, large scale firms in Italy.

Conclusions

Cyclical fluctuations can be ascribed to a great number of causes, depending on which theoretical approach we turn to for an explanation, although some aspects may be common to several approaches. Thus Schumpeter's vision in which economic growth takes the form of fluctuations in the age of capitalism, and is destined to lead to a different type of social organisation, is linked to the theories of Marx. The debate over the very existence of a trade cycle has had alternating fortunes, not only from an analytical viewpoint but also in terms of the nature of the cycle. In fact the phenomenon of stagflation destabilises belief in the cyclical trend, and undermines Keynesian theory and policy prescriptions. However stagflation is short-lived, and so cannot rule out a sudden and more or less co-ordinated deviations from the long-term trend of the principle macroeconomic variables. Indeed alternating periods of prosperity and of stagnation or falling output are quite evident; what may be at issue is the length of the interval. In the neo-classical interpretation of, for example, Wicksell, Schumpeter and von Hayek, the slump is deemed to be essential, in order for the economy to readjust, realign prices and reallocate resources following a boom.

In the cyclical sequence, the relationships between the principal aggregates in the economy intensify, indeed if we could enter

> a cinema in which the characters were economic events, we would behold a curious dynamism. (Pantaleoni, 1907, p. 89)

With this spirit in mind we have examined the principal aspects of the Italian economy, emphasising stabilisation policies in order to highlight the process of development and to underline existing malfunctions, which are more often than not the result of past imbalances.

During the ten years of the so-called «economic miracle», Italy benefited from remarkable synergies between economic, social and political forces; when these disintegrated, the economic boom paved the way for the subsequent impasse. As time progressed, the problems became increasingly impenetrable and the remedies which were experimented met with only partial success. Policy actions and reactions to technical and institutional phenomena ever more and more frequent for historical, social and political reasons. The course of economic events «escaped any kind of monistic explanation». (Savona, 1981, p. 218)

After the reconstruction years Italy experienced the harsh effects of external constraints for the first time in 1963. In the light of such peculiar price dynamics, restrictive monetary and fiscal policies brought inflation in Italy back in line with European levels. In the seventies the Italian economy appeared to embark upon a path of considerable instability, both as a consequence of the changes in labour relations, with the *autunno caldo* (autumn of discountent), and of the related rise in the cost of raw materials. Expectations influenced price formation and fuelled inflation itself, confirming its persistent nature.

We should remember that the long expansionary phase recorded in many countries between 1959 and 1970 was undoubtedly sustained by the intensification of technological progress, although the substantial contribution to development deriving from the application of Keynesian recipes should not be overlooked.

In the seventies and eighties, Italy shared with many other industrialised nations inflationary impulses which emanated from within the internal political and social framework, combined with external inflationary impulses; which created singular situations, in view of Italy's complex and individual reaction to international shocks.

The seventies were marked by the two oil shocks, and the early eighties were years of great uncertainty in terms of the development of the economy, with evidence of a growing number of small firms. A phase of reorganisation and rationalisation of productive processes in middle-sized and large firms, ensued, coupled with the emergence of problems related to employment. The level of employment was strongly influenced by the changing population trends. The progressive ageing of the population in turn gave rise to structural changes in demand for services and manufactured goods, and substantial problems relating to social security and pensions surfaced.

In the eighties the problem of public debt deteriorated, exacerbated by the effects of Ponzi games, and dirigiste incomes policies were introduced in 1984 (the St. Valentine's day decree). The year 1984 marked a watershed in relations between social partners, leading in July to the abolition of the sliding scale, which was held responsible for distorting prices.

In the early nineties, the complex nature of the production crisis could not be explained by the perverse behaviour of demand, hence explanations of Keynesian origin which attributed the responsibility for inflation to aggregate demand were rejected. In this case it was the uncertainty over the nation's political structure which created difficulty, given the inherent fragility of the system itself.

The state of expectations played a crucial role in the development of speculative movements in the nineties in particular, to the extent that the Bank of Italy abandoned its traditional role as "guardian" of monetary stability to deal with frenzied episodes of speculation. As Keynes had warned in the thirties, raising interest rates in order to curb speculation at the end of the trade cycle might seriously damage the economy as a whole. Undoubtedly moral persuasion was unheeded in such a climate of fervid agitation and tempting illusions, so conducive to speculation despite the traps and snares.

Nevertheless the inflationary trend subsequently relented, thanks in part to the abolition of the sliding scale and the start of the process of readjusting public finance in order to comply with the Maastricht parameters. However aggregate demand was insufficient to pull the economy out of stagnation, partly as a result of the general feeling of uncertainty which overwhelmed the country.

Italy approached the new century with structural weaknesses in its employment system stemming from rigidities in the labour market, a tax wedge restraining purchasing power, disappointing output growth and a substantial lack of infrastructures. Statutory regulations also penalised small firms, precisely those firms which had always contributed to the country's positive economic performance by demonstrating an astonishing ability to adapt in the face of fragmentation of output structures and limited international competitiveness. If the new flexibility introduced into the labour market was to expand employment, it was vital to ensure that this did not lead to insecurity in the newly created jobs. In terms of public finance, a reassuring degree of success was achieved, partially due to privatization, although the Public Administration remains is still inadequate in many ways. The financial market is in constant evolution as obsolete legacies are abandoned, although its growing sophistication may have pernicious consequences. In effect

> Financial capitalism has proved to be a powerful factor in creating wealth, and at the same time, to be even more unstable than traditional industrial capitalism. (Banca d'Italia, 2000, *Considerazioni Finali*, p. 36)

The growing use of information technology should lead to substantial growth in knowledge resources, and foster the exchange of information in real time with immediate results in the productive economy. There must be continued faith in the ability of private firms operating in unprotected sectors to adapt to change, a fundamental characteristic which has distinguished private Italian enterprise and one that should certainly not be considered merely a hasty expedient. A global vision calls for a culture based firmly on principles of competition: in a world of increasingly globalisation we must exploit the positive elements in the system and defeat or at least significantly attenuate the negative elements which are inevitable, particularly those which, as we have seen, over time constitute a core and which should not be regarded as an inalienable heritage to be passed on irresponsibly to future generations, but rather as issues to be tackled in a timely fashion with appropriate measures.

References

Given the vast specialised bibliography on the subject, only the authors cited are listed below.

Acocella N. (1995) *Fondamenti di politica economica. Valori e tecniche*, NIS, Rome.

Alesina A. (1987) 'Macroeconomic Policy in a Two-Party System as a Repeated Game', *Quarterly Journal of Economics*, August.

Alesina A. and Drazen D. (1991) 'Why are Stabilization Delayed', *The American Economic Review*, March.

Alesina A., Cohen G.D. and Roubini N. (1997) *Political Cycles and the Macroeconomy*, MIT Press, Cambridge (Mass.).

Alexander S. (1952) 'Effects of a Devaluation on a Trade Balance', *IMF Staff Papers*, April.

Ando A. and Kennickel A. (1986) 'How Much (or Little) Life Cycle Saving Is There In Micro Data?', in Dornbusch R., Fischer S. and Bossons J. (eds), *Macroeconomics and Finance: Essays in Honor of Franco Modigliani*, MIT Press, Cambridge (Mass.).

Andreatta B. and D'Adda C. (1985) 'Effetti reali o nominali della svalutazione. Una riflessione sull'esperienza italiana dopo il primo shock petrolifero', *Politica Economica*, n. 1.

Arcelli M. (2000) *L'economia monetaria e la politica monetaria dell'Unione Europea*, Cedam, Padua.

Arcelli M. and Valiani R. (1979) 'Crowding-out: alcune riflessioni per la politica economica', *Economia Italiana*, n. 2.

Astolfi E. and Negri L. (1993) *Tecnica bancaria*, Tramontana, Milan.

Avagliano L. (1980) *La rivoluzione industriale in Italia*, Minerva Italica, Bergamo.

Bacon R. and Eltis W. (1976) *Britain's Economic Problem: Too Few Producers*, Macmillan, London.

Bagehot W. (1986) *Lombard Street* (*Il mercato monetario inglese*) (1st edn 1873), Italian translation by Einaudi L., CRT, Turin.

Baici E. and Dell'Aringa C. (1994) *L'ingresso dell'Italia nel Sistema Monetario Europeo ed i suoi effetti sul meccanismo di determinazione dei salari*, in Dell'Aringa C. (ed.), *Caratteri strutturali dell'inflazione italiana*, Società Italiana degli Economisti, Rome, 30-31 October 1992, Il Mulino, Bologna.

Balducci R., Candela G. and Scorcu A. (2001) *Introduzione alla politica economica*, Zanichelli, Bologna.

Ball L. (1994) 'What Determines the Sacrifice Ratio?', in Mankiw N.G. (ed.) (1986), *Monetary Policy*, University of Chicago Press, Chicago.

Banca d'Italia (1961) *Assemblea generale ordinaria dei partecipanti. Relazione annuale, 1960*, Rome.

Banca d'Italia (1984) *Assemblea generale ordinaria dei partecipanti. Relazione annuale, 1983*, Rome.

Banca d'Italia (1987) *Assemblea generale ordinaria dei partecipanti. Relazione annuale, 1986*, Rome.

Banca d'Italia (1992) *Assemblea generale ordinaria dei partecipanti. Relazione annuale, 1991*, Rome.

Banca d'Italia (1993) *Assemblea generale ordinaria dei partecipanti. Relazione annuale, 1992*, Rome.

Banca d'Italia (1994) *Assemblea generale ordinaria dei partecipanti. Relazione annuale, 1993*, Rome.

Banca d'Italia (1995) *Assemblea generale ordinaria dei partecipanti. Relazione annuale, 1994*, Rome.

Banca d'Italia (1999) *Assemblea generale ordinaria dei partecipanti. Relazione annuale, 1998*, Rome.

Banca d'Italia (2000) *Assemblea generale ordinaria dei partecipanti. Relazione annuale, 1999*, Rome.

Barca F. and Visco I. (1993) 'L'economia italiana nella prospettiva europea: terziario protetto e dinamica dei redditi nominali', in Micossi S. and Visco I. (eds), *Inflazione, concorrenza e sviluppo.*

L'economia italiana e la sfida dell'integrazione europea, Il Mulino, Bologna.

Barro R.J. (1974) 'Are Government Bonds Net Wealth?', *The Journal of Political Economy*, November-December.

Barucci P. (1969) *Introduzione* to Saraceno P., *Ricostruzione e pianificazione 1943-48*, Laterza, Bari.

Basevi G. and De Grauwe P. (1977) 'Vicious and Virtuous Circles: a Theoretical Analysis and a Policy for Managing Exchange Rates', *European Economic Review*, vol. 10.

Basevi G., Ferrari M., Onofri P. and Poli G. (1993) 'Vincoli di bilancio dell'economia italiana e integrazione finanziaria internazionale', in Micossi S. and Visco I. (eds), *Inflazione, concorrenza e sviluppo. L'economia italiana e la sfida dell'integrazione europea*, Il Mulino, Bologna.

Baumol W.J. (1967) 'Macroeconomics of Unbalanced Growth: the Anatomy of Urban Crisis', *The American Economic Review*, June.

Beckerman W. (1985) 'How the Battle against Inflation Was Really Won', *Lloyds Bank Review*, January.

Beckerman W. (ed.) (1986) *Wage Rigidity and Unemployment*, Duchworth, London.

Bertocco G.C. (1991) *Teoria e politica monetaria nell'analisi della Banca d'Italia*, G. Giappichelli Editore, Turin.

Bickerdicke C.F. (1920) 'The Instability of Foreign Exchange', *The Economic Journal*, vol. 30.

Bilson J.F.O. (1979) 'The Vicious Circle Hypothesis', *IMF Staff Paper*, vol. 26.

Bini P. and Magliulo A. (1997) *The Reception of the «General Theory» in Italy (1936-1963)*, ESHET Conference, 27 February – 2 March, Mimeo, Marseille.

Blanchard O. (1999) 'La disoccupazione in Europa: il ruolo degli shock e delle istituzioni', *Lezioni Paolo Baffi di Moneta e Finanza*, Banca d'Italia, Rome.

Blanchard O. and Watson M. (1982) 'Bubbles Rational Expectations and Financial Markets', *NBER Working Paper*, n. 945.

Blinder A.S. and Solow R.M. (1973) 'Does Fiscal Policy Matters?', *Journal of Public Economics*, vol. 2.

Blinder A.S. and Solow R.M. (1974) 'Analytical Foundations of Fiscal Policy', *The Economics of Public Finance*, Brookings Institution, Washington.

Bodo G. and Sestito P. (1989) 'Disoccupazione e dualismo territoriale', *Temi e discussioni*, n. 123, Banca d'Italia, Rome.

Bodo G. and Sestito P. (1991) *Le vie dello sviluppo. Dall'analisi del dualismo territoriale una proposta per il Mezzogiorno*, Il Mulino, Bologna.

Bodo G. and Visco I. (1987) 'La disoccupazione in Italia: un'analisi con il modello econometrico della Banca d'Italia', *Temi e discussioni*, n. 91, Banca d'Italia, Rome.

Bond M.E. (1980) 'Exchange Rates, Inflation and Vicious Circles', *IMF Staff Papers*, vol. 27.

Bootle R. (1996) *La fine dell'inflazione. Sopravvivere e prosperare nell'era del tasso zero*, Il Sole 24 Ore Libri, Pirola, Milan.

Bresciani Turroni C. (1931) *Le vicende del marco tedesco*, Bocconi, Milan.

Bresciani Turroni C. (1951) *Corso di economia politica*, vol. II: *Problemi speciali*, Giuffrè, Milan.

Bresciani Turroni C. (1957) 'L'economia italiana nel dopoguerra', in *L'economia italiana nel decennio 1947-1956*, Banco di Roma, Stabilimento A. Staderni, Rome.

Bresciani Turroni C. (1978) *Teoria dell'inflazione* (1st edn 1931), edited by Rosati F., Giuffrè, Milan.

Bruni F. (1981) 'Salari: criteri alternativi di indicizzazione in un'economia aperta', *Indicizzazione*, Biblioteca della Libertà, Ente Luigi Einaudi, Turin.

Bruno M. and Sachs J. (1985) *The Economics of Worldwide Stagflation*, Harvard University Press, Cambridge (Mass.).

Burda M. and Wyplosz C. (1993) *Macroeconomia. Un testo europeo*, Il Mulino, Bologna.

Caffè F. (1984) *Lezioni di politica economica*, Boringhieri, Turin.

Cagan P. (1956) 'The Monetary Dynamics of Hyperinflation', in Friedman M. (ed.), *Studies in the Quantity Theory of Money*, The University of Chicago Press, Chicago.

Casarosa C. (1991) *Corso di macroeconomia*, La Nuova Italia Scientifica, Rome.

Caselli P. (1992) 'Fatti stilizzati dell'ultimo ciclo nei principali paesi industrializzati: un confronto con i cicli degli anni Settanta', *Studi & Informazioni*, n. 4.

Cavazzuti F. (1979) 'Il bilancio del settore pubblico allargato: prime linee di un'analisi degli effetti sui prezzi e quantità', *Economia Italiana*, n. 2.

Cencini A. (1995) *Monetary Theory National and International*, Routledge, London and New York.

Cesarano F. (1980) 'L'efficacia della politica fiscale: una rassegna critica', *Rivista di Politica Economica*, July.

Chancellor E. (1999) *Un mondo di bolle. La speculazione finanziaria dalle origini alla "new economy"*, Carocci editore, Bari.

Christiano L.J. (1989) 'Understanding Japan's Savings Rate: The Reconstruction Hypothesis', *Quarterly Review*, Federal Reserve Bank of Minneapolis, Spring.

Chrystal K.A., Faini R. and Guiso L. (1991) *Teorie macroeconomiche. Controversie, fazioni e questioni aperte nel dibattito sulla politica economica*, Hoepli, Milan.

Ciocca P.L. (ed.) (1983) *La moneta e l'economia. Il ruolo delle banche centrali*, Il Mulino, Bologna.

Ciocca P.L. (1987) *L'instabilità dell'economia. Prospettive di analisi storica*, Einaudi, Turin.

Cipolletta I. (1986) *Struttura industriale e politiche macroeconomiche in Italia*, Il Mulino, Bologna.

Cipolletta I. (1990) 'L'industria italiana negli anni ottanta: riflessioni sul cambiamento', *Economia Italiana*, n. 3.

Ciravegna D. (1997) *Elementi di analisi macroeconomica*, UTET, Turin.

Clark C. (1940) *Conditions of Economic Progress*, Macmillan, London.

Clò A. (1992) 'La crisi del Golfo Persico tra cronaca e prospettive', in Bruni F. and Onida F. (eds), *L'economia italiana nel mondo che cambia: 1900-91*, Il Mulino, Bologna.

Cohen J. and Federico G. (2001) *Lo sviluppo economico italiano, 1820-1960*, Il Mulino, Bologna.

Colajanni N. (1990) *L'economia italiana dal dopoguerra a oggi*, Sperling & Kupfer Editori, Milan.

Commissione delle Comunità Europee (1994) *Crescita, competitività, occupazione*, White Book by Delors J., Il Saggiatore, Milan.

Confederazione Generale dell'Industria Italiana (1980) *Terzo rapporto CSC sull'industria italiana*, May, Rome.

Conway R.K., Swamy P.A.V.B. and Yanagida J.F. (1983) 'The Impossibility of Causality Testing', *Special Studies*, Paper N. 178, Division of Research of Statistics, Federal Reserve Board, Washington D.C..

Craig Roberts P. (1984) *The Supply Side Revolution*, Harvard University Press, Cambridge (Mass.).

Dawson G. (1992) *Inflation and Unemployment Causes, Consequences, and Cures*, Edward Elgar Publishing, Aldershot (U.K.).

Deaglio M. (1987) 'Sommersione ed emersione nell'economia italiana', *Economia Italiana*, n. 1.

Dell'Aringa C. (1993) 'Il mercato del lavoro italiano nel contesto internazionale', in Micossi S. and Visco I. (eds), *Inflazione, concorrenza e sviluppo. L'economia italiana e la sfida dell'integrazione europea*, Il Mulino, Bologna.

Dell'Orefice A. (1985) 'Il cambio della moneta: un dibattito fondamentale nei primi anni della ricostruzione (1944-1947)', in Società Italiana degli Economisti (eds.), *La ricostruzione economica italiana dopo la seconda guerra mondiale*, Libraire Droz, Geneva.

Del Vecchio G. (1950) *La sintesi economica e la teoria del reddito*, Cedam, Padua.

Documento Pandolfi (1978) 'Piano 1979-1981. Una proposta per lo sviluppo, una scelta per l'Europa', in Nardozzi G.G., *I difficili anni '70. I problemi della politica economica italiana 1973/1979*, Etas Libri, Milan.

Dornbusch R. and Fischer S. (1992) *Macroeconomia*, Il Mulino, Bologna.

Einaudi L. (1949) *Lezioni di politica sociale*, Boringhieri, Turin, 1958.

Fanno M. (1923) 'Inflazione monetaria e corso dei cambi', off-print, *Giornale degli Economisti e Rivista di Statistica*, 1922-1923, Società Tipografica «Leonardo da Vinci», Città di Castello.

Fanno M. (1935) *I trasferimenti anormali dei capitali e le crisi*, Einaudi, Turin.

Fanno M. (1956) *La teoria delle fluttuazioni economiche* (1st edn 1947), UTET, Turin.

Fazio A. (1979) 'La politica monetaria in Italia dal 1947 al 1978', *Moneta e Credito*, September.

Fellner W.J. (1959) 'Demand Inflation, Cost Inflation and Collective Barganing', in Bradly P.D. (ed.), *The Public State in Union Power*, University of Virginia Press, Charlottesville.

Fink R. (1982) *Supply Side Economics*, University Publication of America, Washington D.C..

Flood R. and Garber P. (1980) 'Market Fundamentals versus Price-Level Bubbles', *Journal of Political Economy*, October.

Fornasari F. (1984) 'Il tasso d'inflazione di base in Italia: stime e proiezioni', *Economia Italiana*, n. 1.

Fortis M. (1988) *Prodotti di base e cicli economici*, Il Mulino, Bologna.

Fortis M. (1990) *Dinamiche settoriali e indicatori di sviluppo. L'economia italiana dal 1950 al 1990*, Il MulinoRicerca, Bologna.

Fratianni M. (1978) 'Inflation and Unanticipated Changes in Italy', in Brunner K. and Meltzer A.H. (eds), *The Problem of Inflation*, Carnegie-Rochester Conference Series, vol. 8, Amsterdam, North Holland.

Fratianni M. (1980) 'Money, Prices and Wages in Italy', *Quarterly Review*, December.

Friedman B. (1978) 'Crowding-out or Crowding-in. Economic Consequences of Financing Government Deficits', *Brooking Papers de Economic Activity*, n. 1.

Friedman M. and Schwartz A.J. (1963) *A Monetary History of the United States, 1867-1960*, NBER, Princeton University Press, Princeton.

Friedman M. and Schwartz A.J. (1965) *The Great Contraction*, Princeton University Press, Princeton.

Galli G. and Nannei A. (1974) 'La base sociale dell'economia bloccata', *Tempi Moderni*, January-March.

Galli G. and Nannei A. (1976) *Il capitalismo assistenziale. Ascesa e declino del sistema economico italiano, 1960-1975*, SugarCo Edizioni, Milan.

Gambale S. (1986) *Economia politica e politica economica e finanziaria*, La Nuova Italia Scientifica, Rome.

Gandolfo GC. (1986) *Economia internazionale*, first volume: *Economia internazionale* and second volume: *Economia monetaria internazionale*, UTET, Turin.

Garavello O. (1977) 'Politica monetaria ed aggiustamento della bilancia italiana dei pagamenti (1947-1975)', in Ranci P. (ed.), *Moneta e politica monetaria in Italia*, Vita e Pensiero, Milan.

Giannone A. (1983) 'Spesa pubblica e sviluppo economico in Italia nel periodo 1960-81', *Note Economiche*, n. 2.

Giavazzi F. and Spaventa L. (1989) 'Gli effetti reali dell'inflazione e della disinflazione', *Rivista di Politica Economica*, July-August.

Goodwin R.M. (1982) 'Teoria delle catastrofi, stabilità strutturale, dinamica qualitativa' (1st edn 1980), in Goodwin R.M. (ed.)., *Saggi di analisi economica dinamica*, La Nuova Italia Scientifica, Rome.

Graziani A. (1972) 'Problemi di politica monetaria in Italia', in Balloni V. (ed.), *Lezioni della politica economica in Italia*, Edizioni Comunità, Milan.

Graziani A. (1979) *Introduzione*, in Graziani A. (ed.), *L'economia italiana dal 1945 a oggi*, Il Mulino, Bologna.

Graziani A. (1997) *I conti senza l'oste. Quindici anni di economia italiana*, Bollati Boringhieri, Turin.

Gressani D., Guiso L. and Visco I. (1988) 'Disinflation in Italy: an Analysis with the Econometric Model of Banca d'Italia', *Journal of Policy Modelling*, n. 2.

Gualerni G. (1980) *Ricostruzione e industria. Per una interpretazione della politica industriale nel secondo dopoguerra 1943-1951*, Vita e Pensiero, Milan.

Guiso L. (1984) 'Il dibattito sull'inflazione italiana negli ultimi 15 anni', *Temi di discussione*, Servizio Studi della Banca d'Italia, n. 38, December.

Guiso L. and Magnani M. (1985) *Perché l'inflazione è calata?*, Banca d'Italia, Rome.

Guiso L., Jappelli T. and Terlizzese D. (1992) 'Why is Italy's Saving Rate so High', *Temi di discussione*, Banca d'Italia, Rome.

Hamilton J.D. (1983) 'Oil and the Macroeconomic since World War II', *Journal of Political Economy*, April.

Hayashi F. (1989) 'Is Japan's Savings Rate High?', *Quarterly Review*, Federal Reserve of Minneapolis, Spring.

Heertje A. and Nardi Spiller C. (1986) *Principi di economia politica*, Cedam, Padua.

Heller W.W. (1967) *New Dimensions of Political Economy*, Norton, New York.

Jossa B. (1991) *Macroeconomia*, with the collaboration of Centorrino M., Cedam, Padua.

Jossa B. and Musella M. (1996) *Macroeconomia: teorie per la politica economica*, NIS, Rome.

Kaldor N. (1959) 'Economic Growth and the Problem of Inflation', *Economica*, August-November.

Kaldor N. (1971a) 'Conflicts in National Economic Objectives', *The Economic Journal*, March.

Kaldor N. (ed.) (1971b) *Conflicts in Policy Objectives*, Blackwell, Oxford.

Kaldor N. (1975) 'What is Wrong with Economy Theory', *The Quarterly Journal of Economics*, August.

Kaldor N. (1986) 'Inflazione e recessione nell'economia mondiale' (1st edn 1976), in Kaldor N. (ed.), *Occupazione, inflazione, moneta e tassazione*, edited by Targetti N., Einaudi, Turin.

Kalecki M. (1975) 'Aspetti politici del pieno impiego' (1st edn 1943), in Kalecki M. (ed.), *Sulla dinamica dell'economia capitalistica. Saggi scelti 1933-1970*, Einaudi, Turin.

Kaminsky G. (1993) 'Is Three a Peso Problem? Evidence from the Dollar Pound Exchange Rate, 1976-1987', *The American Economic Review*, Juin.

Keynes J.M. (1936) *The General Theory of Employment Interest and Money*, MacMillan, London, 1960.

Khaldûn I., sec. XIV, *The Muqaddimah. An Introduction to History*, Princeton University Press, Princeton, 1967.

Kindleberger C.P. (1967) *Europe's Postwar Growth. The Role of Labor Supply*, Harvard University Press, Harvard.

Kindleberger C.P. (1969) *Economia internazionale*, Etas Kompass, Milan.

Kolodko G.W. and McMahon W.W. (1987) 'Stagflation and Shortageflation: a Comparative Approach', *Kyklos*, vol. 40, file n. 2.

Kornai J. (1980) *Economics of Shortage*, North Holland, Amsterdam-London.

Kornai J. (1982) *Shortage and Efficiency: a Macrodynamic Model of Socialist Economy*, Basil Blackwell, Oxford.

Lama L. (1978) *Intervista*, «La Repubblica», the 24th January.

Léon P. (1979) 'Il cambiamento dell'Europa', in Léon P. (ed.), *Storia economica e sociale del mondo*, vol. VI, Tomo I, Laterza, Bari.

Lerner A.P. (1944) *The Economics of Control*, Macmillan, New York.

Lewis W.A. (1954) 'Development with Unlimited Supply of Labour', *The Manchester School*, May.

Lombardini S. (1974) *L'economia italiana al bivio*, Il Mulino, Bologna.

Lucas R.E. (1973) 'Some International Evidence on Output-Inflation Tradeoffs', *The American Economic Review*, Juin.

Lucas R.E. (1981) *Studies in Business Cycle Theory*, Blackwell, Oxford.

Lucas R.E. (1987) 'Models of Business Cycles', in *Yrio Jahnsson Lectures*, Oxford University Press, Oxford.

Lucas R.E. and Sargent T.J. (eds) (1981) *Rational Expectations and Econometric Practice*, Allen & Unwin, London.

Lunghini G. (ed.) (1981) *Scelte politiche e teorie economiche in Italia 1945-1978*, Einaudi, Turin.

Lutz F.A. (1958) 'Inflazione indotta dai costi e inflazione indotta dalla domanda', *Moneta e Credito*, marzo.

Magliulo A. (1998) *Marco Fanno e la cultura economica italiana del Novecento*, Edizioni Polistampa, Florence.

Manoussos G. (1962) *Inflation, Croissance et Planification*, Droz et Minard, Paris.

Marshall A. (1961) *Principles of Economics* (1st edn 1890), Macmillan, London.

Marzano F. (1991) 'La Relazione generale sulla situazione economica del Paese nel 1990', *Mezzogiorno d'Europa*, n. 2.

Masera R.S. (1986) 'Per un risanamento della finanza pubblica in Italia', Banca d'Italia, *Temi di discussione*, n. 61, March.

Mengarelli G.L. (1979) *Politica e teoria monetaria nello sviluppo economico italiano (1960-1974)*, Boringhieri, Turin.

Modigliani F. and Padoa Schioppa T. (1977) 'La politica economica in un'economia con salari indicizzati al 100% e più', *Moneta e Credito*, March.

Modigliani F. and Tarantelli E. (1973) 'A Generalization of the Phillips Curve for a Developing Country', *The Review of Economic Studies*, April.

Modigliani F., Moro B. and Sylos Labini P. (1998) *Sviluppo economico ed occupazione: materiali per un manifesto contro la disoccupazione in Europa*, Franco Angeli, Milan.

Monti M. (1982) 'Promemoria sulle indicizzazioni', *Rivista Milanese di Economia*, July-September.

Morganstern O. (1963) 'Qui Numerare Incipit Errare Incipit', *Fortune*, vol. LXVIII, October.

Mundell R.A. (1961) 'A Theory of Optimun Currency Areas', *The American Economic Review*, September.

Mundell R.A. (1962) 'The Appropriate Use of Monetary and Fiscal Policy for Internal and External Stability', *IMF Staff Papers*, March.

Nardi Spiller C. (1988) 'Nuovi e vecchi problemi accesi dal Cambridge Debate', *Sinergie*, n. 15.

Nardi Spiller C. (1990a) 'Stagflation, dinamica inflazionistica e conflittualità sulle scelte operative nell'esperienza italiana recente', in Gaburro G., Molesti R. and Zalin G. (eds), *Economia Stato Società*, «Studi in memoria di Guido Menegazzi», IpemEdizioni, Pisa.

Nardi Spiller C. (1990b) *Struttura produttiva e dinamica dei prezzi*, introduction by Baranzini M., Cedam, Padua.

Nardi Spiller C. (1991a) 'L'esperienza dell'Unione Monetaria Latina nel sistema monetario internazionale', *Il Pensiero Economico Moderno*, n. 3.

Nardi Spiller C. (1991b) 'Luzzati e l'Unione Monetaria Latina', *Credito Popolare*, n. 5.

Nardi Spiller C. (1992) 'L'andamento del corso dei cambi e la dinamica inflativa nell'analisi di Marco Fanno', in Manfredini Gasparetto ML., ed., *Marco Fanno. L'uomo e l'economista*, Cedam, Padua.

Nardi Spiller C. (1993) 'Le fluttuazioni economiche: punti convergenti e divergenti tra l'apporto di Fanno e il contributo di altri studiosi', in *Atti della giornata di studio dedicata a Marco Fanno*, Mediocredito Centrale, Rome.

Nardi Spiller C. (1994) *La dinamica inflativa nell'economia italiana dal secondo dopoguerra agli anni Novanta*, Cedam, Padua.

Nardi Spiller C. (1996) *Il passato prossimo della teoria economica nel dopo Keynes*, Cedam, Padua.

Nardi Spiller C. (1997) 'E' la fine dell'inflazione nell'UE', in Savio G. (ed.), *Dalla Comunità Economica Europea verso l'Unione Europea: Problemi e prospettive per il futuro*, vol. 5, Cedam, Padua, 2000.

Nardi Spiller C. (2000a) 'Affinità e distinguo nell'analisi delle fluttuazioni cicliche tra Fanno e Hayek', *Nuova Economia e Storia*, n. 1-2.

Nardi Spiller C. (2000b) 'L'integrazione monetaria europea: l'esperienza della Lega Latina', *Rivista Bancaria – Minerva Bancaria*, n. 5.

Nordhaus W. (1975) 'The Political Business Cycle', *The Review of Economic Studies*, April.

O'Connor J. (1973) *La crisi fiscale dello Stato*, Einaudi, Turin.

OECD (1980) *Italy*, March, Paris Cedex.

Olivera J. (1967) 'Money, Prices and Fiscal Lags: A Note on the Dynamics of Inflation', *Banca Nazionale del Lavoro - Quarterly Review*, September.

Olsen M. (1982) *Ascesa e declino delle nazioni. Crescita economica, stagflazione e rigidità sociale*, Il Mulino, Bologna, 1984.

Onida F. (1974) *La bilancia dei pagamenti come vincolo alla politica economica*, Franco Angeli, Milan.

Onida F. (1993) 'Collocazione internazionale e fattori di competitività dell'industria italiana', in Micossi S. and Visco I., (eds), *Inflazione, concorrenza e sviluppo. L'economia italiana e la sfida dell'integrazione europea*, Il Mulino, Bologna.

Padoa Schioppa F. (1990) 'Classical, Keynesian and Mismatch Unemployment in Italy', *European Economic Review*, n. 41.

Pantaleoni M. (1907) 'Una visione cinematografica del progresso della scienza economica (1870-1907)', in Bocciarelli R. and Ciocca P.L. (eds), *Scrittori italiani di economia*, Laterza, Bari, 1994.

Parkin M. (1978) 'Alternative Explanations of U.K. Inflation: a Survey', in Parkin M. and Summer M. (eds), *Inflation in the U.K.*, University Press, Manchester.

Parkin M. and Bade R. (1991) *Macroeconomia moderna*, Italian edition edited by Spinelli F. and Tirelli P., Etaslibri, Milan.

Parkinson C.N. (1980) 'Parkinson's Law (1st edn 1955), in Mansfield E. (ed.), *Managerial Economics and Operations Research*, W.W. Norton, New York.

Pasinetti L.L. (1996) 'L'onere sociale degli alti tassi d'interesse', in Cozzi T., Nicola P.C., Pasinetti L.L. and Quadrio Curzio A. (eds), «*Studi in onore di Siro Lombardini*», Vita e Pensiero, Milan.

Pasinetti L.L. (2000) 'Public Debt in the European Union Countries: Two Ways of Facing the Problems', in Krishnakumar J. and Ronchetti E. (eds), *Panel Data Econometrics: Future Directions*, «*Papers in Honour of Professor Pietro Balestra*», Elsevier, Amsterdam.

Pendersen L. and Karnosky D. (1977) 'A Monetary Interpretation of Inflation', *National Bureau of Economic Research*, Washington.

Pittalunga G.B. (1999) *Economia monetaria. Moneta-Credito. Attività produttiva*, Hoepli, Milan.

Pizzini E. and Nardi Spiller C. (2003) 'Dinamica dei prezzi nella Germania riunificata: impatti sul meccanismo europeo', in Savio G. (ed)., *Dalla Comunità Economica Europea verso l'Unione Europea: problemi e prospettive per il futuro*, vol. 7, Cedam, Padua.

Podbielski G. (1974) *Italy, Development and Crisis in the Post-War Economy*, Oxford University Press, Oxford.

Poole W. (1970) 'Optimal Choice of Monetary Policy Instruments in a Simple Stocastic Macro Model', *Quarterly Journal of Economics*, May.

Predetti A. (1990) *Temi di metodologia della politica economica*, Cisalpino, Milan.

Prosperetti L. (1993) 'Struttura e politica industriale: l'esperienza degli anni ottanta e le questioni aperte', in Micossi S. and Visco I. (eds), *Inflazione, concorrenza e sviluppo. L'economia italiana e la sfida dell'integrazione europea*, Il Mulino, Bologna.

Rampini F. (2000) *New Economy*, Editori Laterza, Bari.

Ricardo D. (1954) *Principi dell'economia politica e delle imposte con altri saggi sull'agricoltura e la moneta* (1st edn 1817; 2nd edn 1819; 3rd edn 1821), edited by Fubini R. and Campolongo A., introduction by Loria A., UTET, Turin.

Robinson J. (1950) 'The Foreign Exchanges' (1st edn 1937), in Ellis H.S. and Metzler L.A. (eds), *Readings in the Theory of International Trade*, Blakiston, Philadelphia.

Rostow W.W. (1959) 'Rostow on Growth', *The Economist*, the 15th of August.

Rostow W.W. (1960) *The Stages of Economic Growth*, University Press of Cambridge, Cambridge (Mass.).

Saba A. (1980) *L'industria sommersa. Il nuovo modello di sviluppo*, Marsilio Editori, Venice.

Salvati M. (1975) *Il sistema economico italiano: analisi di una crisi*, Il Mulino, Bologna.

Sarcinelli M. (1981) 'Il ruolo della banca centrale nell'economia nazionale', *Economia Italiana*, n. 3.

Sargent T.J. and Wallace N. (1981) 'Some Unpleasant Monetarist Arithmetic', *Federal Reserve Bank of Minneapolis*, Autumn.

Savona P. (1981) 'Considerazioni sullo stato della modellistica economica in Italia: note a margine dei due modelli CSC', *Economia Italiana*, n. 2.

Schultze C.L. (1959) 'Recent Inflation in the United States', Work Document by the Joint Economic Committee, *Study of Employment, Growth and Price Levels*, n. 1, Government Printing Office, Washington, 1959.

Scitovsky T. (1978) 'Market Power and Inflation', *Economica*, August.

Sennet R. (2000) *L'uomo flessibile. Le conseguenze del nuovo capitalismo sulla vita personale*, Feltrinelli, Milan.

Shapiro C. and Stiglitz J.E. (1984) 'Equilibrium Unemployment as a Worker Discipline Device', *The American Economic Review*, Juin.

Siesto V. (1987) 'Statistiche macro-economiche ed economia irregolare', *Economia Italiana*, n. 1.

Signorini L.F. and Visco I. (1997) *L'economia italiana*, Il Mulino, Bologna.

Smith A. (1975) *La ricchezza delle nazioni* (1st edn 1776), Italian translation by Bagiotti A. and T., biographical note by Pellanda A., UTET, Turin.

Solow R.M. (1956) 'A Contribution to the Theory of Economic Growth', *Quarterly Journal of Economics*, February.

Spinelli F. (1976) 'The Determinants of Price and Wage Inflation. The Case of Italy', in Parkin M. and Zis G. (eds), *Inflation in Open Economics*, Manchester University Press, Manchester.

Spinelli F. (1980) 'Italy and the Cost Push Hypothesis: a Critique of Ward and Zis, Laidler and Hibbs', *Journal of Monetary Economics*, n. 3.

Spinelli F. and Fratianni M. (1991) *Storia monetaria d'Italia. L'evoluzione del sistema monetario e bancario*, Arnoldo Mondadori Editore, Milan.

Spinelli F. and Tullio G. (1982) a cura di, *Saggi di politica monetaria e fiscale in Italia*, Ceep/Franco Angeli, Milan.

Spinelli F. and Zis G. (1979) 'The Wage-Inflation-Unemployment Trade-Off in Italy: a Critique of Modigliani and Tarantelli', *Economic Notes*, n. 1.

Sraffa P. (1960) *Produzione di merci a mezzo di merci. Premessa a una critica della teoria economica*, Einaudi, Turin.

Stammati G. (1975) *Il sistema monetario internazionale*, Boringhieri, Turin.

Stevenson A., Muscatelli V. and Gregory M. (1988) *Teorie macroeconomiche e politiche di stabilizzazione*, Monduzzi Editore, Bologna, 1992.

Sylos Labini P. (1970) 'La "gelata di primavera"', *L'Espresso*, the 12th of April.

Sylos Labini P. (1972) *Sindacati inflazione produttività*, Laterza, Bari.

Sylos Labini P. (1982) *Lezioni di economia*, vol. II, Edizioni dell'Ateneo, Rome.

Sylos Labini P. (1983) *Il sottosviluppo e l'economia contemporanea*, Laterza, Bari.

Tanzi V. (1977) 'Inflation, Lags in Collection and the Real Value of Tax Revenue', *International Monetary Fund Staff Papers*, March.

Thurow L. (1996) *The Future of Capitalism. How Today's Economic Forces Will Shape Tomorrow's World*, N. Brealey, London.

Thurow L. (2000) 'Intervista', *Corriere della Sera*, the 16th of March.

Triffin R. (1947) 'National Central Banking and the International Economy', edited by Board of Governors of the Federal Reserve System, *Postwar Economic Studies*, n. 7, Washington.

Triffin R. (1961) *Gold and the Dollar Crisis*, Yale University Press, New Haven.

Trigilia C. (1992) *Sviluppo senza autonomia. Effetti perversi delle politiche nel Mezzogiorno*, Il Mulino, Bologna.

Tsoukalis L. (1997) *La nuova economia europea*, Il Mulino, Bologna.

Vaciago G. (1975) 'Credito totale interno e offerta di moneta', *Rivista Internazionale di Scienze Sociali*, September-December.

Vaciago G. (1990) 'Debito pubblico e mercati finanziari', in Arcelli M. (ed.), *Politica monetaria e debito pubblico negli anni Ottanta in Italia*, UTET, Turin.

Vaciago E. and Vaciago G. (2001) *La new economy. Un modo nuovo di fare ricchezza*, Il Mulino, Bologna.

Valiani R. (1979) 'La finanza pubblica', *Economia Italiana*, n. 1.

Valli V. (1990) *Politica economica: i modelli, gli strumenti, l'economia italiana*, La Nuova Italia Scientifica, Rome.

Valli V. (1993) *Politica economica*, first volume: *Teoria e politica dello sviluppo*, La Nuova Italia Scientifica, Rome.

Valli V. (1999) *Politica economica europea, Macroeconomia e politiche di breve periodo*, Carocci editore, Rome.

Verri P. (1910-42) 'Carteggio di Pietro e Alessandro Verri' (1st edn 1770), vol. IV, edited by Greppi E. and Giulini A. [after edited by Novati F. and Seregni G.], Cogliati L.F. [after Giuffrè], Milan.

Vito F. (1946) *Problemi economici del dopoguerra*, Giuffrè, Milan.

Wagner A.H.G. (1912) *Les Fondaments de l'Economie Politique* (1st edn 1876), Girard & Brière, Paris.

Wynne M.A. (1999) 'Core Inflation: a Review of Some Conceptual Issues', *ECB Working Paper Series*, May.

Name Index

Subject Index

GPSR Compliance

The European Union's (EU) General Product Safety Regulation (GPSR) is a set of rules that requires consumer products to be safe and our obligations to ensure this.

If you have any concerns about our products, you can contact us on ProductSafety@springernature.com

In case Publisher is established outside the EU, the EU authorized representative is:

Springer Nature Customer Service Center GmbH
Europaplatz 3
69115 Heidelberg, Germany

Batch number: 10725973

Printed by Printforce, the Netherlands